Always Climb Higher!

Jeff Pagels

Always Climb Higher!

This writing is dedicated to my wife Jane, and our sons, Corey and Chad. Without their amazing help, I would not have survived the past 30 years.

Table of Contents

Introduction - How Did I Get Here?

Well this is interesting, I thought to myself. Here I am hanging by a rope under a snow cornice, just inches away from being on top of the highest mountain in the lower 48 states, Mount Whitney. When I swivel my neck I can see Death Valley shimmering 14,000 feet below.

It has been an awesome three days of climbing higher and higher in my sit ski rig. My guide, Kurt Wedberg is using his shovel and a big booted foot to knock a hole in the snow cornice so I can pull myself on top. Nevertheless, for now I have to endure a steady cascade of cold snow in my face and down my neck. How did I get here and what is a sit ski?

To start this story, I need to go back to the late 1800s in Manhattan, New York. There was an outbreak of tuberculosis and people were sick and dying all over the city. In this area, the one small tuberculosis sanatorium was critically overloaded with patients. The doctors decided that people who had a chance to live would be housed in the hospital. Others, who they predicted would die, were to be housed in tents with cots on the hospital grounds. It was the best they could do with limited resources.

Astonishingly it took only one year before doctors realized that patients in the tents were living longer than those in the hospital. Some might say that this was due to unsanitary conditions in the hospital, something that could be still documented in many parts of the world today. But, others, like me, use this story to highlight the value of living your life outside. Those of us who are fond of this precept like to say that being **Outdoors is Strong Medicine!**

Up until the age of 34, my life was fairly unremarkable and typical. I grew up in Manitowoc, Wisconsin. I married high school sweetheart, Jane, went to college and graduated from the University of Wisconsin Stevens Point. Jane and I entered the Volunteers in Service to America program, (VISTA) in Michigan's Upper Peninsula. Vista was and still is the domestic Peace Corps. We were young and naïve, full of optimism to make things better for so-called poor people. I am afraid we did not accomplish much of our goal.

But I was the one who learned a lot from "da Yoopers". They may have not had money but they were rich in so many other ways.

We eventually ended up in Green Bay, Wisconsin; Jane in nursing and me working for the Wisconsin Department of Natural Resources. We had two young boys, Corey and Chad, a dog and a mortgage.

One fateful weekend in 1984, I traveled up north for three days of grouse hunting and chores at our family's cabin near Mountain, Wisconsin. It was a foggy misty Friday afternoon and we were cutting trees next door at Uncle Dick's cabin. That is where I got my label disabled.

Chapter 1 - A Ruined Weekend

The plan was simple. Our task was to cut down a three-pronged White Birch tree next to a screened porch at Uncle Dick's cabin We had a rope hooked up to a Jeep and as I sawed, Dad's friend Bobby, who was driving, was to pull the tree down and away from the porch. This worked well for the first two trunks of the tree.

As I started to cut the remaining branch, a light misty drizzle started falling. The old jeep was equipped with four balding tires. We attached the rope and I began cutting a notch in the remaining log. Once I started cutting through the main section of wood, it did not take long for the tree to start falling.

Bobby started to back up when a strange thing happened. The tree started turning on itself, wrapping the rope and pulling the jeep towards me rather than away. I sensed trouble and started running. I don't know why, but in a split second, I decided to try running around the screen porch. That split second decision turned out to be an almost fatal flaw. As I reached the far side of the porch, the tree crashed into the roof and fulcrumed over to the other side. A branch about the size of a baseball bat slashed my left ear and hit with such a force on my shoulder that my spinal cord and five ribs blew up. Medically speaking I had completely severed my spinal cord at T12 to T10 and fractured five ribs. "T" refers to the Thoracic or mid back level in the spinal cord. The lower the number, the closer to the skull and the more damaging the injury. T10 paralysis starts about the level of the belly button.

I collapsed in a heap with the still running chain saw buzzing loudly in my ear. I realized, with terror, that I could not breathe. I saw my father, Ray, standing over me, and just before I was going to black out, I was able to take a small breath. Finally I could breathe. I vaguely recall asking Dad to turn the chainsaw off and straighten my legs, noting his perplexed expression.

My lower back was very sore and I thought straightening my legs it would relieve the pain. He quickly turned off the saw and moved it away from my head but seemed confused by my request to straighten my legs. At that time

I glanced down to notice that my legs were indeed positioned straight out from the rest of my body.

That is when the realization sunk in that I'd been seriously injured. Dad encouraged me to get up, so he could help me get to our cabin to lie down on a bed until I felt better. I had to tell him, however, this was serious. I could not feel anything in my legs and he'd better go get some help.

In this remote part of Wisconsin's Northwoods, the nearest telephone was across Highway 64 at Bobby's cabin. No one had cell phones in 1984. Bobby ran to make the 911 call. It took about 20 minutes for the ambulance to arrive. By that time I was in a lot of pain and apparently going into shock. The light rain was now a steady downpour.

The ambulance pulled up in a field about 50 yards from where I lay, but as they tried to get closer they got mired in soft ground. The ambulance was stuck and stuck good. One of the ambulance attendees stood out on Highway 64 with Bobby, waiting for a four wheel drive vehicle with enough power to pull the ambulance free, to come down the highway. The first responders didn't want to put me in the ambulance until it was ready to roll, so I waited on a stretcher with a blanket over me as the minutes ticked by. It was nearly a half hour before a suitable vehicle came along and was stopped. It took short work for them to pop the ambulance out of the mud and in no time at all I was on my way to see a doctor in Mountain, a small village six miles away.

When we arrived, I remember looking up at the doctor as I grabbed his tie to pull him in closer. In a not so polite voice I asked him, eye to eye, to give me a painkiller. He was reluctant to do so at first, but with the death grip I had on his necktie, I convinced him to give me a shot of something to lessen the pain.

From Mountain, I was transported to the nearest hospital, 30 miles away, in Oconto Falls. I was admitted to the emergency room while Dad called Jane. She was on her way and would be there shortly. He did not tell Jane the severity of my situation. He told Jane that I injured my shoulder.

In the examination room, the medical staff quickly realized they did not have the resources to take care of a severe spinal cord injury. Back in the ambulance I went for about another 50-mile ride to Saint Vincent's Hospital in Green Bay. Earlier that day, Dad and I dined on green pea soup with ham sandwiches, for lunch. I am not sure if there was a specific medical reason for it, but as we sped down the highway towards Green Bay, I spewed pea soup all over myself, Jane, the floor and part of the ceiling. To this day Jane will not make or eat green pea soup! But I still like it!

When I arrived at Saint Vincent's, it was another trip to the emergency room and then the intensive care unit. After undergoing X-rays and a CT scan my official diagnosis was determined. It did not take long for the doctor to tell me my back was broken and I would not walk again. In many stories this is the point where the hero insists that despite the doctor's prediction that he will walk again. That's not what I did though. I knew in my heart the doctor was right. The reality and details of what lay ahead had yet to sink in, but I was already planning for my new view on life.

Well, it seemed that I had cheated death and was safely being watched in an intensive care unit in a sophisticated hospital. With Jane at my bedside and hooked up to a bunch of monitors, I must've fallen asleep. Did I dream? I don't remember, but I do remember to this day, the nightmares that were to come in the weeks ahead.

Chapter 2 - False Terrors

It might have been day two or three or four, for that matter. My mind is unclear on the sequence of events after the first night. I do remember that Jane stayed by my side most of the time. I also remember getting large doses of morphine to reduce the pain and I recall asking to be able to see some wheelchair users. Two guys in wheelchairs came to see me one day for about 30 minutes. In the months ahead, both would become close friends and confidants. But on that day, I just wanted to see what a wheelchair user really looked like up close and personal. They seemed like normal people.

I learned I had to stay in the ICU until my vital signs stabilized enough to undergo major surgery to repair my back. The surgeon needed to install metal rods in my back and keep them in place with bone shavings from my own hip.

There were some lighter times in the ICU, though. A funny story that stands out in my mind involves Jane's help caring for me and a poignant lesson learned about the workings of medical equipment. Depending on the medications I was receiving, I either had a very dry mouth or a very wet one. One night, I needed to spit, so Jane held a metal pan beneath my chin. As the pan rested on my chest, it connected to two different sets of electrodes that set off an alarm on the monitors at the nurse's station. Suddenly the room was swarming with nurses and technicians who all figured I was flat lining which is fancy medical talk for dying. Oh well, we learned not to connect electrodes with metal again!

Eventually, I was ready for surgery, which apparently went off without a hitch. Since Jane was a nurse she knew most of the medical personnel around Green Bay and she asked Dr. Alan Wentworth to be the lead guy in the operating room. After I woke up I was ready to start the healing process.

As I mentioned earlier morphine was my painkiller of choice but after about two weeks, the green slime nightmares started to occur. These nightmares had me walking down a sidewalk but melting into a pool of green slime flowing into the cracked sidewalk, over the curb, down the street and into a sewer over and over again. No pain could be worse than these visions that haunted me. I stopped the morphine.

Chapter 3 - The Rehabilitation of Me

Eventually I was relocated to a regular room on the recovery floor in the hospital. For a while I had a roommate, later I had a private room. My roommate was a high school football player who had a bruised liver.

Probably the worst pain I endured came several weeks after the tree cutting incident when it was discovered that I had five broken ribs which had become infected. The painful part was that I could not take a breath without excruciating burning pain in my ribs. I was forced to lie flat on my back and take shallow, shallow breaths. This went on for several days. Talking was out of the question as was eating or drinking. But, eventually the infection was stopped and I was transferred to the rehabilitation ward at St. Vincent's. This was my first event with an infection that required the use of antibiotics. But it was not the last event and it might someday be the very last event in my life.

As I remember it, I was the only spinal cord injured person on the rehabilitation floor. Most of the other patients were stroke victims. Early on, I was visited by different "mental counselors" as I like to call them. One of them was a quadriplegic with a power chair that predicted I would in no uncertain order get a divorce, lose my job and that I should hopefully like to read books because reading was one of the few things I would be able to continue to do. (A quadriplegic has a spinal cord dysfunction that involves both the arms and legs.) For many years afterward I took this guy to task every time I had the opportunity. He failed to realize that I was not a quadriplegic; that I still had the use of my arms and my upper body. And that history would bear out that I did not lose my job and I did not lose my family and I did much more than just read. (Not too long ago I stopped despising this person as I finally realized it was a waste of my energy.)

While in the hospital I worked at my job with the Wisconsin Department of Natural Resources (DNR) for four hours every day. This allowed me to cut my sick time use and was something that would become very valuable to me in my retirement years. This was at the beginning of the computer age and the Department's tech specialist, Bruce Miller, came to my room and set a computer up which allowed me to communicate with people and continue my work around Northeast Wisconsin. This was my first real entrance into the electronic age and is something I embrace even now. I am still not too good at it, but I still embrace it! Jane was my mail carrier, taking and bringing paperwork to the DNR office.

The other hours in the day were set for rehabilitative therapy and visits from friends, family and well-wishers.

Chapter 4 - How to get out of the hospital after breaking your back

After the incisions healed and ribs mended, it was time to get on with planning an escape. At first, therapists came to my room to have me do minimal exercises with tiny dumbbell weights. One recollection I have of this is dropping a weight on the floor and the resounding loud percussion set off spasms through my spinal cord that were very painful. I planned never to drop another weight on the floor! Also, every time I saw a football game on TV the bone crunching tackles made me cringe.

Eventually I became strong enough to go to the therapists instead of them coming to me. One major difficulty was becoming able sit up straight. The summer before my injury I competed in a lot of triathlons. These are events where you swim a certain distance like 1 mile, bike 26 miles, and then run 6 miles to complete the race. I was probably in the best shape of my life and my legs were huge with well-developed muscles. Now my body was working against me because as I attempted to sit up straight blood would pool in those now placid muscles. Every time I tried to sit up it was either pass out or feel like throwing up.

The way you become acclimated to standing up was a torturous device called a standing table. Therapists would lay me on a table and strap me in and then crank the table towards a standing position until I either got sick or started to faint. This was done every other day and was the low point of the rehabilitation. When the human body suffers from lack of exercise and activity, it begins to wither away and so did eventually my legs. It took about a month, but finally I was able to tolerate a standing table and sitting up in a wheelchair.

A note about wheelchairs. People say all the time that it would be horrible to be in a wheelchair. I need to look at it in a different way. If someone had not invented wheelchairs, where would I be? The ability to move around and in many cases move faster than other human beings is something that I welcome. My life revolves around adaptation. It takes a lot to keep me alive and moving around and it's because science and individuals have made improvements that allow me to continue on living a decent life. In my situation the good old days were not great because suffering a spinal cord injury 50-60 years ago was usually a death sentence.

At night in St. Vincent's, Jane would find a wheelchair some place. I would get into it and push up and down the halls trying to gain back some arm strength and coordination. Over the years I got pretty good at using a wheelchair. I was at least better than a lot of the able-bodied friends who tried to get in my chair and do wheelies at our house. The walls and floors and my friends heads all took a beating while the rest of us laughed.

By my definition, Physical Therapists work on getting your body healthy. Occupational Therapists help you teach your body to do things like dress, eat, drink, push a wheelchair, get back into a wheelchair once you fall out, transfer from your wheelchair to a car, drive a car, and all the other things that go into living life sitting down in a stand up society.

One of my projects in occupational therapy was to build a transfer board. This thing was about 24 inches long and 10 inches wide and one inch thick. My job was to smooth the board so it did not have any slivers, then varnish and re-sand the board until it was smooth. The purpose of the board was to aid in the transferring from one wheelchair to another or from wheelchair to a bed or automobile. That is all I remember about occupational therapy while I was at Saint Vincent's hospital. But, I still have and use the board on a daily basis.

At physical therapy I tried always to outdo my therapist's recommendations and challenges. If they'd tell me to do 10 arm curls with a dumbbell I would do 20. Once they were comfortable with me doing 20 and saw that I could indeed handle 20 I would do a 30. I would always try to do more than they asked. And, I continued to chew up and spit out mental therapists.

Jane had hand controls installed in our Dodge Caravan and without any instruction I jumped in one afternoon and started to drive. Except for almost taking out the disabled parking sign at a Red Lobster restaurant, my driving with hand controls became second nature.

Back in the 1980s, it was typical for a spinal injured person to spend six to eight months in a hospital and rehab center. Nowadays patients are discharged in a matter of a few weeks. In my case I got out in three months. That was considered amazingly fast. In fact, the insurance company sent a nurse to see if I truly had a complete spinal cord injury because they could not believe I had gotten out of the hospital so quickly.

After being discharged I visited the hospital for outpatient therapy and to council other spinal cord patients that were coming onto the floor. But the hospital did not appreciate what I had to tell them. My message was simple; leave Saint Vincent's and transfer to Craig Spinal Cord Hospital in Denver, Colorado. I had a chance to spend some time at Craig the summer after my accident. I learned more in one week there than I learned in three months at Saint Vincent's. I learned how to take care of myself and use a wheelchair. I also learned of the hazards of being a spinal cord injured person with regard to bladder and bowel matters and pressure sores. Believe me; not being able to walk is one of the least of the worries of living life in a wheelchair.

Chapter 5 - Getting on With Living

Jane had reluctantly left her good nursing job working for a Podiatrist. She was my right hand helper in so many ways. I may have escaped the hospital in just three months but I could not have done it without Jane.

Before I left Saint Vincent's Hospital for good, I was allowed to go home one day for several hours, then for an entire day and eventually overnight. Since the elevator was not done yet, I had to butt my way up the stairs to the bedroom. Steve Bannow built a set of steps that I also butted up to get level with my wheelchair. Then I would transfer from the steps to the wheelchair. Lastly it was one more transfer to get from the chair to the bed. All that work was worth it to sleep in my own bed.

Jane and I also were allowed to leave the hospital on little adventures like going to eat in a restaurant. Among the many get well cards we received while in the hospital, there were a fair number of gift certificates for restaurants in the area. We enjoyed taking trips for lunch to these restaurants, which is something I fondly remember. These mini-adventures helped me to get acclimated to the new normal slowly. I highly recommend restaurant gift certificates for newly injured friends.

I also recall taking several trips to go archery hunting for deer while still living at the hospital. On one trip to Waupaca County with my Father, I actually sat in my wheelchair on the edge of the woods. It was a cold, blustery, bright sunny day. It was not a good day for hunting, but I was out there and I even saw a deer about ½ mile away in a field. It would be several years before I developed decent enough skills to kill a deer from a wheelchair.

On another trip, a friend, Steve Bannow, took me up to the deer yards in Florence County Wisconsin. It was a long ride in his pickup truck and when I got there I spent the entire time taking a nap on the seat of his truck. I was too wasted to actually get out and hunt. But it was good to be away from the hospital and in the deep, snowy woods. In fact until this day it is no secret, at least not since this book came out, that I like to take naps in the woods. I know my sons and some friends shake their heads in disappoint-ment but I bet the deer and turkey appreciate the naptime as much as I do.

Meanwhile, at my house a cadre of volunteers were working long hours to ready the home for a wheelchair user. We live in a four level house with three levels of stairs plus steps into the house. Improvements included a ramp in the garage that led into the house, widening doors and making space under sinks for my wheelchair to fit. A remote garage door opener was installed in the garage.

The most expensive project was an elevator installation to link me to all four floors. It was a huge undertaking. The only thing not done by volunteer help was the inspection of the wiring by a Village of Ashwaubenon building inspector.

To save on expenses I remember traveling with friends late one chilly afternoon to pick up the elevator. It was about a one-hour ride to Waupaca Elevator in Waupaca, Wisconsin. The elevator parts were in a bunch of boxes. On the way home, four of us were jammed in the front seat of the van with the elevator parts taking up every available space including sticking out the rear doors.

The money to pay for the elevator and other home improvements came from a fundraiser friends had one night at the Association for Retarded Citizens Center in Green Bay. It was a huge deal that netted over $19,000 in donations. This allowed us to pay for the garage door opener, a combina-tion snow blower - riding lawn mower tractor, and house remodeling as well as the elevator. If you come into our home and the elevator doors are shut you would never know that there was even an elevator in the place. It is very well concealed. The guys had to knock a hole in the roof to make the elevator fit. On the weekend that they did this our house was exposed to the winter elements. It was only a matter of about an hour after they enclosed the roof than a huge snowstorm hit. As they say, timing is everything!

A good friend over all these years, Tom Noth, has faithfully maintained the elevator. The machinery is as good is now as it was 30 years ago. Tom has been over any and all hours during the day or night to service it. I've had several clumsy moments in the elevator where I became trapped because I had broken something. Early on I had a telephone installed so I could call people if I was home alone and stuck. The phone has proven invaluable except for one time...sort of.

One day during the middle of a Packers football game on TV, I happened to go into the elevator for some reason during a commercial break. Somehow, something stopped functioning and I was trapped. I called around to various friends with no success. I finally found one friend, Jim Wallen, who was home watching the game. Jim taught me a valuable lesson about the cult status of the Packers. It was an important game and there was only about one quarter left to be played. Jim said he would be over after the game was completed. So, there I sat for about 30 minutes in the elevator with one ear glued to the door listening to a television in the adjoining room. It's funny now, but like many things it wasn't at the time it happened!

Speaking of the Packers, I had a few other interesting developments with these professional football players. When I got injured in the Fall and ended up in the hospital I had been painting our house all summer long. I still had at least half the house to paint. At that time I was coaching youth soccer with the Packers Chaplin, Steve Newman. Steve contacted the head coach and he agreed to send the entire team over one afternoon to finish painting. All the ladies in the neighborhood brought food and the kids were there to help do what they could and to seek autographs.

The Packers finished our house in record time and it was another chore I could drop off my list of things to do. That same night, the Packers Wives Club held a scavenger hunt for the team. One of the places each Packer had to go to pick up a clue was in my room at the hospital. So, it was a never-ending stream of Packers showing up in the room. Between the two events I collected many autographs plus an autographed football.

The third memory of the Green Bay Packers was the donation of a racing canoe by Packers wide receiver James Lofton valued at $800. James wanted to do something individually to help me out. Since Jane and I had been canoe racers much of our lives, I intended to try and get back in the sport once I was healed up.

Before my injury I had started taking college courses to earn a master's degree at the University of Wisconsin-Green Bay. I was taking one course a semester. After my injury I really was not too sure where my life was headed. Now I not only continued to take college courses I jumped up to a full load of classes. I attended school most nights and weekends. I was awarded a master's degree in environmental public administration in 1986. I graduated with straight A's but besides bragging rights, I am not sure the added degree added anything to my salary level.

The campus was very accessible including a swimming pool that I could get into. This rekindled my interest in swimming and swimming fast. I was on my high school swimming team and at my first college, in Stevens Point. In fact, I was the team captain and made All-American one year.

I remember one day in the swimming pool locker room another fellow in a wheelchair was getting dressed. I never have mastered getting dressed while sitting in my wheelchair. I knew people could do it but 99% in my dressing I was lying down on a bed. It made getting dressed a lot easier, if there was a bed or a table that I could jump on. This guy was preparing to put on his underwear; I watched with rapt attention to see how he did it. Much to my surprise and dismay when it came time to put on the underwear he stood up! Obviously, he was not as disabled as I was! That is just one of the tricks of the trade I did not learn over the years about living life as a wheelchair user.

At the DNR office where I worked accommodations were also provided that made working conditions more accessible. My desk was raised with blocks so I could fit under it comfortably. One of the bathrooms was completely gutted and a lock put on the door that made it very accessible and usable for me and others. One of the biggest enemies to a wheelchair user are narrow spaces and the stalls existing before remodeling provided insurmountable barriers. By simply taking out all the stall walls, and putting a lock on the door I was able to get in there and do what I had to do.

I also was given the opportunity to use my own vehicle for official travel. The typical rate for employees to be paid for official use of their vehicles was about 20¢ a mile back then but I, as a disabled user, was allowed 50¢ a mile, which I thought, was a pretty good deal. But I kept detailed records of all my expenditures and soon learned that 50¢ a mile did not cover all the expenses when I used the vehicle for work purposes. So, eventually I asked for and was assigned a personal vehicle to use.

One day while in Madison, the State Capitol of Wisconsin, attending a meeting, I was interviewed by various state employees about workplace accommodations for the physically disabled. They were looking for ideas to take back to other parts of the State. The disabled population of state employees was growing and accessibility and the Americans with Disabilities Act was becoming something everyone was talking about. After awhile, one of the questions turned personal.

I specifically remember one question where a woman said "Jeff, you seemed to be handling your disability quite well. You seem to have a good attitude. Is there anything that gets you down?" I hesitated for a moment before answering. I told them that one of the hardest things to accommodate was the fact that I could not cross country ski anymore. And that was true. Corey, Chad, Jane and I liked to cross country ski race almost every weekend during the winter.

While in the hospital I agreed to become a coach for kids under the Bill Koch Youth Ski League program. In reality this never happened. On Friday nights I would help my sons prepare their skis for the Saturday race that they were planning to go to. But, when the Saturday morning came, I would look out the window at the snow and just could not bring myself to leave. It was too devastating to realize I was no longer going to be able to cross country ski.

As I shared this sad tale with the group, a guy in the back stood up and raised his hand. I could tell when he stood up that he was blind. He wore dark glasses and had a red and white cane. He told the group and me that I could in fact learn to ski again. He indicated that he attended a program called Ski for Light that paired him with a sighted volunteer who would guide him on ski trails for miles and miles. The blind guy told me that they also had a program for mobility-impaired skiers. They used a sort of sled and small ski poles to move down the trails. After the meeting I rolled over to talk with him and got more information about this amazing revelation.

Chapter 6 - Ski for Light - The Early Years

I went to my first Ski for Light (SFL), in January of 1986. My last event was in 2005. For 19 years I gave my heart and soul to this program; but SFL gave it all back to me and more. It was the beginning of my real journey out of doors.

On a crisp, cold sunny morning I left Green Bay for Duluth, Minnesota, a drive of 5 hours. I found the hotel and checked in. There were a couple hundred people in the dining room having dinner as I snuck by and headed to my room, where I pretty much hid for the next hour or so. Eventually there was a knocking at the door and somebody introduced themselves as being with SFL. Later my roommate entered. He was a wheelchair user like me but sad to say I don't remember his name. I just remember that he stiffed me the $20.00 that I loaned him toward the end of the week.

The next day, I met some people that would become lifelong friends. The magic of the SFL program soon engulfed me. In the mornings we played on an ice rink with adaptive ice skates and in the afternoons we attempted to ski on these red plastic sleds using very short ski poles. It was tough. We also had a lot of fun at a local ski area going downhill instead of cross country.

In order to ice skate we would sit on a sled with a chair that had hockey skates welded to it. We used short ski poles equipped with metal tips that dug into the ice. It was a lot of fun as you can get moving quite fast on good ice. They happened to play on an area of a local lake that was plowed free of snow. The frozen surface was not that great but I got the idea that this sport could be a lot of fun.

Alpine skiing was done at Spirit Mountain, a very nice downhill ski area near Duluth. We downhill skied because the art of cross country skiing by wheelchair people had not been refined enough to make it much fun. So while the blind people cross country skied at a city park we segregated ourselves at Spirit Mountain.

A typical American SFL program was patterned after a program in the country of Norway called the Ridderren. It consisted of about 100 blind or visually impaired skiers with an equal number of sighted guides and from five to twelve mobility impaired skiers plus guides. Usually the team of two became fast friends not only for the event but for the rest of their lives. One important concept I learned here was the fact that the guides or the volunteers or the helpers in most cases had more fun, more appreciation and more understanding than those being helped. I am fond of saying it this way: "if you think it's fun to catch a fish wait until you help someone else catch a fish."

Besides all day outside activities, each night saw numerous activities going on in the hotel. The food was amazing as well as the camaraderie. There was so much going on I did not want to waste time sleeping. But sheer exhaustion finally made the sleep come easy. In later years I told others that they could sleep on the plane ride home after the week was over.

One thing I had not mastered as a wheelchair user was dancing. Jane and I loved to dance but since my accident that was another thing that had gone undone. I learned to dance in Duluth Minnesota! This learning curve was not without mishap however. One night after maybe one too many beers I was doing a wheelie in front of the band. I tipped over backwards and took out the entire drum section and the music stopped abruptly. I think I was somewhat embarrassed! I don't remember a lot more about the week except that it just went by really fast. I do remember coming home. I held Jane very tightly for a very long time with tears of joy and jabbering on and on about what had happened up in Duluth Minnesota. It was truly life changing.

The next winter Ski for Light was held in Traverse City Michigan. Again, I was able to drive to the event but this time I took Jane along. The plan was for Jane to guide a blind skier and I again participated in the mobility impaired program. We again had a downhill ski area but this time due to lack of ice there would be no skating. Traverse City had something that Duluth Minnesota did not, an outside hot tub. Over the years having a hot tub at Ski for Light became the rule rather than the exception. This was a place after a long day outside where broken bodies could heal up and warm up at the same time. Plus the social interactions were amazing. We are fond of saying that we solved all the world's problems in the hot tub.

Jane was a gamer. She had a less than great experience at this event guiding a girl from Detroit Michigan who had mental issues besides not been able to see. Jane's skier was very afraid of the concept and probably for the entire week did not ski more than one kilometer total. Jane would take her out every day but it was a challenge. One day a friend of mine who lived in Lower Michigan stopped by to say hello. John Weimer became enthralled with the program and after that accompanied me as a guide for the program for many, many years. Jane also was a guide for quite a few years before deciding that Ski for Light was something she could do without.

Traverse City was a breakthrough in that I finally learned how to master cross country skiing in a more exciting way. And this is how it happened.

One day, later in the week I went out skiing with Jane and her skier. At that time I was using my yellow downhill pulk. The pulk is a flat bottom sled that I sat in to slide down ski hills. I would steer myself by dragging my hands, shifting my weight on either side depending on which way I wanted to go.

For propulsion on the ski trails I used some short ski poles. It was exhausting but I could keep up because Jane's skier only made these tiny little baby steps going just a few feet. At some point on the trail one of my little ski poles broke in half. I was a long way from the ski shelter where I had left my wheelchair. Seeing no other alternative, I asked Jane and if I could borrow her ski poles. It is possible for a standup skier to cross country ski without the use of poles. But for me without the use of my legs I was going nowhere fast.

Jane's poles seemed way too long for my outstretched arms but a phenomenal thing happened when I started to pole. I literally shot down the trail. It was one of those "Aha" moments. The secret to cross country sit skiing as I now realized was the length of the poles. Before this my ski poles probably came up half way up to my chest. Now I realized that poles of several inches above my head as I sat in my pulk were optimum. I could actually move down the trail in a speedy fashion and on top of that it just felt great cardiovascular and muscle wise.

Chapter 7 - Wheelchair Road Racing & Basketball

In the early days of rehabilitation for spinal cord injured, two sports stood out. They were wheelchair road racing and wheelchair basketball. I had to try both and I learned after awhile that I was miserably inept at both.

While I was in the ICU at Saint Vincent's hospital, another friend of mine, Winter Hess challenged me. Winter challenged me to do a wheelchair marathon as soon as I was able. The marathon distance is 26.2 miles. I accepted the challenge and I worked hard to accomplish it. Before my injury I had done a couple marathons including a race in Chicago. About 365 days after my injury I successfully completed the Chicago marathon in a wheelchair.

One recommendation you probably will not find in rehabilitation manuals is the need for the injured person to have a backyard mechanic. A backyard mechanic is someone who can build anything. I had a backyard mechanic and still do. His name is Bob Joslin. Over the years Bob has built me a myriad of adaptive gear used to make my life easier and more fun. I used to tell Bob; "You build them and I drive them." Over the years I continue to use that phrase as I am not mechanically inclined.

One of the first projects Bob took on was to build me a racing wheelchair.

Back then these chairs did not look at all like a conventional wheelchair as they had large front wheels that were eventually replaced with just one front wheel. The push rims were much smaller than the conventional rims on a standard wheelchair. Guys that were good at it can really make these contrivances fly. Like I said earlier I was not good at it. Bob and I looked at pictures of racing wheelchairs in magazines and that's all we used to fabricate mine. On the first chair he did miss one adaptation that we realized later on was very important and that was a tie rod system.

On one of my first attempts on the road with my new chair, I started going downhill and picking up speed. As the speed increased the two front wheels on the chair started to shimmy. Soon the entire chair was shaking uncontrollably and I flipped over and over and over down the street. Gosh, did I accumulate a bad case of a road rash. On that wheelchair we learned the hard way about the need for tie rods. My next chair had a tie rod system that prevented the chair from shimmying.

The Chicago marathon was pretty exciting. It just so happened that about half way through the race I was caught by the cars, motorcycles and photographers following an Olympic runner Joan Benoit. All the hoopla and excitement of the lead woman runner swept me along and I was able to hold my pace with Joan the rest of the race. I did not win the race but I finished and was pleased.

During the next few years I went through a series of improved wheelchairs for racing and did several other marathons and shorter road races. One of the most important and exciting races I was involved in was in 2008 in Green Bay.

The Bellin Hospital 10 K run is one of the largest running events of its kind in the United States. As is the norm, runners have started after wheelchair racers or more recently hand bike racers. Besides knowing these are disabled individuals who cannot run, not much else is known about these athletes with disabilities.

Some of the race watchers might know that these athletes start in front of the runners because most of them are faster than the fastest runners on the course. In fact, while the course record for a runner was 27:46, the course record for a disabled chair or hand bike racer was under 23 minutes!

In most years, usually only one of the disabled racers moved out at a high rate of speed, but in 2008, three of the disabled hand bike racers carried on a very hotly contested race that for the most part went un-noticed by race watchers.

Keith Lenns, Dave Samsa and I brought to the starting line a mix of age, technology, race smarts and physical ability. This eclectic mix resulted in no less than seven lead changes during the 6.2 mile course.

Keith had never before won a hand bike race. Keith was in pretty good shape as a result of running his own construction company even though he has been using a wheelchair since 1996 as a result of a car accident.

Dave, who was 43, had won the Bellin hand bike division three times before. He became a wheelchair user as the result of a car accident over ten years ago. (An errant driver crossed the center line and hit Dave head-on.)

I was probably the most experienced racer of the three and had the most modern hi tech hand cycle, but also was the most out of shape.

A hand cycle is an adapted bicycle that is propelled by arm power by those that can't use leg power. They range from lower cost/fewer speeds, (under $2,000) to 27 plus speed high Tec machines costing as much as $10,000. In the past, many wheelchair using athletes raced in wheelchairs but have moved to hand bikes because they are easier on the shoulders, elbows and wrists. Many race organizers will not allow hand bikers into running races for a variety of reasons or excuses. We gave many thanks to the Bellin organizers for recognizing the reasons why disabled athletes use bikes instead of wheelchairs to enter the Bellin.

The 2008 Race: An hour before race time, Keith and Dave were warming up on their hand bikes, which is the smart thing to do. I was going to do the same, but discovered a mechanical problem with my bike and had to spend precious minutes trying to figure out what was wrong and then fix it. (Remember, I don't build them I just drive them!) Just minutes before the race, the bike was fixed and I only had time to get to the start line and race.

I decided to start in a mid range gear and move up to the high range once the speed got up over 12 miles an hour. When the gun went off, Dave and Keith took off, (apparently already in high gear) with me already 15 yards behind only 50 yards from the start.

The first mile of the race is a subtle up hill on Webster Avenue that can kill a racer who starts out too hard. After I jumped to a high range gear, I quickly passed Keith and got right behind Dave. I was able to hang in Dave's shadow by drafting. Even though I was gasping for any extra oxygen in the air, I was able to save precious energy by not having to work as hard as Dave and was able to recover and somewhat lower my redlining high heart rate.

In the 2007 race, I watched Dave gain a huge lead on the Greene Street downhill, so about 100 yards before the left turn; I passed Dave for the lead. The lead did not last very long as Dave regained the lead by a no-fear no-brakes all out flash downhill heading toward Green Isle Park. By the Green Isle Park turn, Dave had a 100 yard lead over the more cautious me and looked like he would add another first place award to his life list. I did not want to count myself out just yet and set out to again try and catch Dave. And, where was Keith? I figured he was way behind and nothing to worry about.

Unbeknownst to Dave, I was slowly gaining ground and unbeknownst to me, so was Keith. By the time Dave turned off Libal Street, I had caught back up and was once again drafting him figuring to hang there until the final turn and then make another pass and take the gold. About half way up Hastings Street at about the 5.3 mile mark Keith had done the near impossible and caught both Dave and myself, passing by looking strong. I made the decision to leave Dave and try to hang with Keith and did catch him just after the turn on to Clay Street which was a nice gradual downhill.

Here is where I made a fatal mistake by making a move to pass Keith to take the lead instead of waiting until closer to the finish. When I passed Keith, I figured he dropped way back, but I was wrong again as Keith dropped in behind me and drafted in my wake. At the very last turn at Porlier and Webster Street, Keith made a last ditch move and passed a very surprised me who had no time to react and quickly dropped 20 yards behind as Keith crossed the finish line two seconds ahead of me. Dave came in third a few moments later. What a race even if very few onlookers knew the details as described above.

For most of my life I had been a keen competitor who raced at the world class level. But, this Green Bay race was probably the most competitive event in my history of racing.

Wheelchair basketball

The other recreational pursuit encouraged by rehabilitation experts was wheelchair basketball. This type of basketball has the same rules as able bodied basketball. The only exception is that the player with the ball can take up to two pushes with their wheelchair in between dribbles. Pushing down the court with the ball resting in the lap would be considered "traveling" and therefore not legal.

There was no wheelchair basketball program in Green Bay when I was injured. But with other wheelchair friends I had made along the way, including those two that I met in intensive care, Carl Schott and John Leilou the Northeast Wisconsin Horizons wheelchair basketball team was formed.

At that time there was a league in Wisconsin with wheelchair basketball teams found in Eau Claire, Milwaukee, Madison and, Lacrosse besides our team here in Green Bay. Periodically we would travel to these other cities to compete. Besides other wheelchair basketball teams we also played what were called "celebrity" teams. For instance, one night we played physical therapists from around the city at a local high school gymnasium. Another time we traveled to team member Steve Boney's home town, Wabeno, to play the able-bodied high school basketball team. Those games displayed the prowess of wheelchair athletes and served to open the eyes of the able-bodied spectators on what we could do.

Our basketball team never lost one of those celebrity games. An interesting sidelight to our travel to other cities to play wheelchair basketball was the fact that quite a few members of our team had never been out of Northeast Wisconsin and were downright rookies when it came to staying in hotel rooms and fending for themselves in restaurants or gas stations.

We usually traveled with some able-bodied volunteers who helped unload wheelchairs as well as any other chores needing done that we could not do ourselves. I myself had done a lot of traveling for a long time and it was rewarding for me to help other team members who did not have a clue about life away from Green Bay.

Jessie Pontzlaff was a quadriplegic who was on our team. Jesse had extremely minimal use of his arms and hands. His major role on the court was to block other teams from getting to the ball. But every game we gave him and Steve who had Cerebral Palsy an opportunity to try and make a basket. Unfortunately neither of them ever did make a basket but, at least they tried.

As I said earlier we never lost a celebrity basketball game, however; we never were able to beat another wheelchair basketball team as long as I was playing. After a couple years of being involved in the team I retired and moved on to other competitive sports where there was one on one competition. Individual competition is interesting in that you can take all the credit or accept all the blame for how you placed in the race.

Chapter 8 - Swimming and Winning

I started my competitive swimming career at Manitowoc Lincoln High School. I did OK on an OK team. I also swam at UW-Stevens Point where I did pretty well on a great team. I became team captain and awarded the "Most Valuable Swimmer" accord in my junior year. I set some records and was elected to the University's Athletic Hall of Fame some years after graduation.

Swimming is a healthy lifetime sport and I took to the water like a fish after my injury. Many wheelchair users develop a healthy fear of the water, but not me. I had no problems in an aquatic environment.

It did not take long after leaving the hospital that I started to include swimming in my therapy regime. And, after that it did not take long to realize that there was competition available to people like me in the pool.

The first thing I did not understand was that I had to be classified. There are many different levels of ability in disabled athletes. And, out of a sense of fairness, participants are classified in an attempt to have like disabilities compete against each other. For instance, a one leg amputee would be racing against other one leg amputees. Blind swimmers would race against other blind swimmers. And the same goes for wheelchair athletes; the higher the injury in your back the lower your classification. It would not be fair for me to swim against a quadriplegic that would have a much more difficult time in the water than I would. Thus I would swim against others with similar spinal cord injuries.

Let's get one thing straight that I am not a pretty sight when I swim. I flail a lot, my butt sticks out and my lifeless legs and feet sink down. I figure I swam about the same pace as a five year old able-bodied kid. In wheelchair road racing, wheelchair basketball, skiing, ice hockey and hand cycling sometimes being a wheelchair user has a technological advantage over the able bodied. But this is not the case in swimming. All that is relative when both swimmers with similar disabilities are trying to beat each other; it is still a race.

I used to train Green Bay area pools. When Corey and Chad were on the Green Bay YMCA swimming team I would get up early in the morning and attend their practices at the Broadview YMCA. It was grueling to get up at 3:00 AM but when I came out of the locker room after getting dressed I felt invigorated. Those were days I felt I accomplished a great deal.

As I started to compare my times against national records of other swimmers with my disability I began to realize that I had a fighting chance to break some records. The first opportunity occurred during the summer of 1985. Jane and I flew to Los Angeles California to attend the National Wheelchair Swimming Association meet. We swam in the famous outside pool at the Santa Clara swim club. We were the new kids on the block. As seems to be typical of competition it was hard to break into the circle of people who knew each other but did not know me. I decided to let my swimming do my talking for me.

I remember more about the trip like driving to San Francisco along the ocean front, driving over the Golden Gate Bridge, and going out on the expansive fishing piers into the Pacific Ocean. But, toward the end finally we got together with the swimmers at somebody's house. While Jane and I ate corn on the cob without salt or butter, (not so good but that's how they did it) others were getting high on marijuana. I want to set the record straight… we did not participate in the drug sessions. But, it sure opened our eyes to a seedier side of athletics.

For the next several years, we took our family vacations around the country based on where the national swimming meet was being held. We had a popup camper that we dragged along behind our van. We had the camper custom made by Amish people in Indiana. So after a fashion it was wheelchair accessible. But, it took an able bodied person to put it up and take it down. Before we sold it Jane had the task of taking care most of that with some help from our sons. All I could do was sit and supervise, which did not sit well with Jane.

One summer we drove to Houston Texas and after that down to Galveston where we camped on the Gulf of Mexico. One day Corey , Chad and I were playing in the ocean and a wave knocked my glasses off. It was the only pair I had. Just by dumb luck Corey swam around and actually found them for me. Corey had a knack of doing that on occasion the last time being up in Canada when his canoe tipped over.

Another summer, we drove east to attend a meet in Philadelphia. After that we headed further east to camp on the Atlantic Ocean at Assateague National Lakeshore Park. This is a park right on the ocean that had wild ponies. If we had a window open in the camper, you could almost certainly plan on a pony sticking his head in looking for a snack. We kept the windows shut tight when we were not in the camper.

One day when playing around in the ocean surf I was hit by a wave that pushed me backwards onto the beach. As you know I don't have any control over my legs. The waves pushed one of my legs up over my head and behind my shoulder just like a contortionist. Corey and Chad had to untangle me as I looked like a pretzel!

One day, we watched an old man net tasty crabs on a bridge attaching the campground to the mainland. We took some spare screening from our camper, string and a chunk of bacon and fashioned our own crab trap. All we caught were small ones that we had to toss back as it did not meet the minimum size regulations. But we found an easier way to eat crab.

There was all you can eat crab place not far from a campground where they put newspaper on the table a bib around your neck and a small wooden mallet to bust up the crab shells. What a messy dinner that was and we worked so hard to get those pieces of crab meat I doubt if we gained many calories.

Jane and I also flew to Rhode Island one year for competition and I flew alone to Erie Pennsylvania one year for competition. I was getting better at swimming and maybe more importantly I started having friendships with quite a few swimmers. I became a founding member of U.S. Wheelchair Swimming the national governing body for swimming for people with disabilities. My biggest achievement was getting U.S. Wheelchair Swimming incorporated as a nonprofit organization. Maybe I should have grown up to be a lawyer because over the years I've done lots of things that lawyers get paid big bucks to do.

In 1989 the Pan-American games were hosted by Caracas, Venezuela and the U.S. was sending a team of disabled athletes including swimmers. After some qualifying meets I and others were chosen to represent the USA in Caracas. This was an exciting trip having never been to South America before. I do remember a couple of interesting tidbits.

One, wherever we traveled we were under armed guard. I got used to seeing people in uniforms watch you with sub-machine guns. I also remember eating lots of bananas or dishes that included bananas. One day while playing tourist downtown I ordered a hamburger and it came with a fried egg on top, it was pretty tasty!

 Nothing nasty ever happened to us... well almost nothing. One day we were riding an escalator up out of the subway area in downtown Caracas when a thief ripped the earrings right off one of our assistant coaches and swallowed them. That coach and another coach tackled the guy and pinned him to the floor awaiting the local police who came and arrested the guy. And the coach eventually did get her jewelry back, after the guy passed them a few days later. I am not sure she ever wore those earrings again I don't think I would have.

Other than that one altercation Caracas seemed to be a very peaceful city but with very diverse cultures. In the middle of the city, which was sur-rounded by steep hilltops, everyone seemed to be quite affluent. But, on the hillsides not far away from where we stayed you could see the shantytowns perched precariously on steep slopes. Lots of the shanties seem to be made of metal sheeting or cardboard. I'll never forget that view.

At the swimming pool I was on a relay team with three other swimmers and I also swam the 50 meter breaststroke in the 50 meter butterfly both of which I had taken first place. The butterfly was a world record at that time for my disability. It was a stroke not many people with my disability could master. But my previous college swimming experience gave me an apparent advantage.

After each finals race the competition organizers were presenting medals to the winners. We had a young girl who was a quadriplegic and, she had won a gold medal in one of her races. When the winning racer was given their medal a loudspeaker blared the national anthem of that particular country for a brief time.

In the case of this girl when they started to play the national anthem the recording malfunctioned. A bunch of us started singing the national anthem. People in the stands also started singing and soon it was very loud and boisterous. So instead of just a few seconds of our country's national anthem we sang the whole thing loud and clear. It made me proud to be an American.

One more negative note happened one night. My roommate and I came back to our hotel room only to find the door knob, door and floor covered with vomit. We learned later that some of the USA athletes who were wheelchair road racers had gotten very drunk and did all sorts of vandalism including the vomit on our door. Another sad display of the negative antics of so called world class athletes.

It was customary at the University of Wisconsin Stevens Point to annually have an alumni swimming meet. I had attended a few other of those meets before I was injured. This time I went to swim as a wheelchair swimmer. To make a statement I did something no swimmer in the past or since has attempted to do. I swam every event in the meet including the relays. I of course swam slow at my typical five year old pace but I swam my heart out and no one has had the courage try and do it again since I did it.

My oldest son Corey, followed me to Stevens Point and the swim team. He was a great swimmer in his own right and lettered all four years that he was there. It just so happened that the coach that I had, Red Blair, was still on campus and coaching when Corey arrived. Coach Blair retired and they threw a big party for him which we attended. You could either buy T shirt that said," I swam for Red" or "My kid swam for Red". By then I was associated with the JanSport Corporation, a company that printed shirts. The company president, Paul Delorey had some special shirts printed up for Corey and me. Corey's read, "Me and my dad swam for Red". And my shirt read, "Me and my kid swam for Red". Those shirts were the hit of the party.

At about this point in my life I was also starting to make a statement in the cross country ski venue. I had planned to participate in both sports because one was a summer time sport and one was winter. And cross training has always been a good way to stay in shape. But the official's at U.S. Wheelchair Swimming would have none of that. They told me I had to decide if I wanted to be a swimmer or a skier. I could not do both in their eyes. So I made a decision which then and even now seems to have been the right one. I said goodbye to my wheelchair swimming friends and headed for the ski trails.

Chapter 9 - Ski for Light - The Middle Years

Back in the 1990s, Ski for Light preferred to move around the country to different venues. This was done to give different segments of the Country's disabled population easier access to the event. In recent years, the event has usually stayed on the western side of the United States including Alaska. Ostensibly this was because the west seems to have better snow conditions and hotel complexes are large enough to accommodate the group, which exceeds 250 in a normal year.

In 1987, Ski for Light was held in Fairley Vermont. I flew to Boston a few days early and was then given a ride up to Fairley by a friend who we had met in Traverse City Michigan, Claire Morrisette. Both Claire and I were on what was called the "Planning Committee". It was a group of volunteers that planned and implemented the annual Ski for Light event.

I was asked to get involved in the Mobility Impaired Program (MIP) after the event in Traverse City. The former event coordinator was not able to attend the event in Vermont thus opening the door for me to get involved even more. This would be my second trip to Fairley, as I also attended a planning meeting out there in the fall of 1986.

During the preceding summer, Bob Joslin, my backyard mechanic, and I developed a relatively cheap and durable ice sled. We had sent 20 of them out to Vermont for the event. In these early years we propelled the sleds with short and sharp pointed ski poles. It did not take much to break the poles, so evenings were spent repairing them to use again the next day. (We eventually changed over to much stronger and safer wooden sticks with a hockey stick on one end and a series of short spikes on the other.)

Once again our ice was natural in the form of a lake adjacent to the hotel complex. It was good that the lake was frozen because there was hardly any snow left on the ground when Ski for Light convened its week-long event.

The planning committee did their darnedest to create opportunities for the blind people and guides to pass the time why we waited for it to snow. One of the big hits was everyone using the ice sleds out on the lake. In fact some say it saved the event. We did get some snow for the last two days of the event but it was too little and too late.

I also continued to work with my friend Steve Bannow to improve the sit ski design by adding cross country skis to the frame and raising it up a bit off the snow. We also added a knee brace that allowed me to sit in a more comfortable position. This thing had really started to let me ski fast and I displayed my prowess with it at the Vermont event by beating lots of blind skiers in the week ending race on the last Saturday. The sit ski was especially fast on the icy conditions that we had. Standup skiers had to contend with slipping and sliding as I just zipped by them under almost total control!

I must digress a bit back to late winter 1986. Steve Bannow's first prototype was made out of PVC pipes that were glued together. We took this ski frame out to a nearby elementary school athletic field. I sat on the frame and started to push myself through the snow. I got about 75 yards from where Steve and my wheelchair were waiting. All of a sudden the frame completely came apart into just a pile of plastic. We learned that lesson the hard way. We needed to make the frame of something other than PVC pipes that were glued together.

How did I get back to my wheelchair you might ask? It could have been a dicey situation had I been alone like I was prone to do on future solo ski trips. But this time, Steve just hiked across the field with a red sled and pulled me and the pile of pipe back to the parking lot.

One more digression. I credit Steve Bannow with being the Father of the modern sit skiing design. I can never thank him enough for all the brain-power and mechanical aptitude he put into this project. At one point we had it in our minds to mass produce the sit ski frame and sell them. However, Steve's wife Diane was skeptical and nervous about liability issues. Because of that Steve had to drop out of the project. But he had done enough that others like me were able to carry on. I went on to sell over 100 of the ski frames. I used the profits from those sales to improve the MIP program at Ski for Light.

It was customary every year for the Ski for Light organization to send two skiers and two guides to the country of Norway for a huge disabled ski event called the Ridderren. This was where Ski for Light has its roots.

At the final gala banquet in Fairley, much to my complete surprise, I was selected as one of the skiers to attend the Ridderren in Norway. My guide, Tip Ray, was to help me participate in the races to be held at the event. Jane and I quickly decided that both she and our two young boys would come with me to Norway. None of us had ever been overseas before. Little did I know that I would go to the beautiful country of Norway a dozen times over the years to come.

A few weeks later we turned U.S. greenbacks into Norwegian kroner, packed our bags and flew from Chicago to Amsterdam to Oslo Norway. After a couple of days touring Oslo we boarded cars driven by the elite "Kings Guard" regiment of the Norwegian Military. It was about a 5-hour drive up winding roads to Beito, a small ski village, way up in the mountains. Once there we had a wonderful week of cross country and downhill skiing with other mobility impaired participants as well as my immediate family and rapidly growing Ski for Light family.

Well, I should footnote that it was a wonderful week after the first day. At the ski area I jumped into my sit ski and strapped myself in. There was this not so high snow bank to go over to reach the trails. What I did not realize that there was a concrete curb hidden underneath the snow bank. I plowed into it and busted off one of my ski tips. I did not have an extra pair skis a long and it never crossed my mind that I could do this kind of damage. I eventually found a different pair of skis that we were able to use on my frame and the week was saved.

One of the competitive events at the Ridderren was the biathlon. This was a race where the competitors shot at targets with a .22 caliber rifle and then skied around the course repeating the shooting at certain intervals. This is a sport where mind over matter can make or break you. After tearing around the course at top speed the competitor needs to quickly settle the breathing down so the targets can be hit.

I always was comfortable wielding a rifle and that expertise paid off in the biathlon. Much to the surprise of the Norwegians I won that event with a perfect shooting score. My skiing wasn't that fast but my excellent shooting scored more points than their fast skiing and I won my first gold medal.

My American guide for the week Tip Ray had been very capable in helping me whenever I needed help. Tip and I have maintained sporadic contact over the years but really renewed our friendship with a five day kayaking trip off the Lake Superior Apostle Islands in the late summer of 2011.

One of the stories we laughed about went like this. During the last ski race of the Norwegian Ridderren, Tip and I started off together like we usually did. But the race was long and the conditions for a sit skier were perfect. It did not take long before Tip had a hard time keeping up with me. As the finish line approached about ½ mile away I picked up speed and left Tip behind. I can still recall his mournful yelling of "Go Jeff Go"!

During this last race I placed in fourth just out of the gold, silver and bronze medals. Much to my surprise at least two of the Norwegians that bested me were rolling handmade cigarettes and lighting them up as I crossed the finish line. I vowed to myself that that would not happen again. No, I was not going to take up smoking - I just was not gonna let somebody who is smoker beat me ever again. The next time I returned to Norway those guys never had a chance as I left them in the dust in every race we had. Truth be known, it was not whether they smoked it was the length of my ski poles and the fact that my ski design allowed my knees to be bent instead of extending out straight. It was not long before ski racers all over the world were designing frames with bent knees. Thank you again Steve Bannow.

Chapter 10 - Continuing To Ski Towards Gold

Another Ski for Light able-bodied friend that I had made in Duluth Minnesota, Harlan Hanson invited me to Mora Minnesota in 1988 to race in a 30 km ski race called the Vasaloppet. Harlan was also connected with the United States Disabled Ski Team as he guided blind skiers in other races around the country. I did not realize that other members of the team were also in the Vasaloppet that day. At this point there were no sit skiers on the disabled ski team. All of them were either blind or amputees.

To make a long story short, with Harlan skiing at my side, I beat all the blind skiers and a couple of the amputees in this race. To make the day even better, my youngest son, Chad took 3rd in his age group.

I stayed in contact with the coaches of the U.S. ski team and eventually was invited to West Yellowstone Montana to participate in a Thanksgiving week ski camp. Up until the day I left for the camp, I debated with myself about if I should go down this path or not. I was not sure how much of my life I wanted to devote to skiing fast. I'm not recalling all the details of what went into my decision-making, but the final decision was to go for it.

West Yellowstone ski camp was held in conjunction with the able-bodied national ski team as well as elite collegiate and master's skiers from around the country. In the cross-country ski community I was in some pretty heavy-duty company.

One of the neat things we did besides skiing in west Yellowstone was to go into the local school system and talk to kids about our sport and our disabilities. Over the years I've had several opportunities to do this in different parts of the country including Washington, DC. It was always a thrill for me to talk with kids of all ages. Besides talking in the classrooms, we skied with the kids outside after school. One day we held a huge relay race. Each team consisted of two disabled ski team members, two able-bodied ski team members and two kids. The yelling and screaming was heart stopping.

Our coaches tried to toughen us by taking us out on predawn runs around the community. Most of the time the air temperature was below zero. There was plenty of whining by team members except me. I always was a "morning" person. I thought the time outside like this was exhilarating and really made me hungry for breakfast.

It just so happened that the hotel we stayed in, the Three Bears Lodge, had a hot tub. That was good news. The bad news was the hot tub was down a flight of stairs consisting of about 40 steps. I and the other chair users would butt ourselves down the stairs quite fast and then jump in the hot tub. After 45 minutes or so of soaking in 104° water the trip back up the stairs one step at a time was one hell of a workout. But, we all felt it was worth it.

One difference between the disabled and able ski teams is worthy of note. The able-bodied ski team essentially skied, ate, and slept the entire winter away. They had very few diversions. On the other hand, disabled ski team members skied on weekends on their own time and just the time at training camp. All of them had jobs and college educations. So, at camp, when we were not skiing or resting we usually on the phone back to our offices or companies catching up on what needed to be done. I think that made us fresh and not as prone to become stale. I think the disabled ski team members were hungrier than the able-bodied counterparts. It's hard to say how we would it turned out had we been fulltime, seven day a week, all winter long professional ski racers.

I sort of set the ski team administrators back on their rear ends at a roundtable discussion one night with the coaches and medical staff. Each skier was supposed to introduce themselves and tell why they were at this training camp. All the regular old timers were first and I was last. One said he was there to get in shape. One said she was there to learn how to ski better and faster. One said they were there at Yellowstone and to meet up with old friends and rekindle relationships. Eventually it was my turn. I told them I was at West Yellowstone to win a gold medal in the next Paralympics.

My statements earned me a ride back to Bozeman Montana, from where we flew home, by the team psychologist. He explained to me that I was maybe setting my sights too high and therefore setting myself up for failure. Once again a so-called expert on my mind was messing with me. I concluded two things on the drive down to Bozeman. One that there was someone in the car who was a failure and two it was not going to be me.

My first world cup competition was in Jackson New Hampshire in 1990. Skiers from all over the world came to Jackson in the first World Cup competition ever held in this country for disabled cross-country skiing.

This was my second exposure to the international level competition and I did OK. My first race was 10 kilometers or 6.2 miles long, and I placed quite a ways down the leader board. The coaches were good number crunchers and I was able to look in detail at my per kilometer splits for the entire race. One thing became apparent to me was that I was not in the best of shape. As a race wore on my splits got longer and longer. In fact had I been able to maintain my initial splits on a more consistent basis I could have been in the medals.

 My second race was half the distance of the first only 3.1 miles long. I was doing very, very well until I spun out on a sharp turn before a bridge. I wasted precious seconds righting myself and getting back on the track and ended up in fourth place just seconds off the bronze medal winner. Dang it! This competition whetted my appetite to ski better and faster. I trained with a vengeance spring, summer, fall and winter for two solid years before the 1992 Paralympics in Albertville France. About the only thing I lost during that time period was weight!

I continued to go to Thanksgiving ski camps in Bozeman Montana and to the national championships at various places around the country including Anchorage Alaska, Rumford Maine and Royal Gorge California. I lost count of how many medals I won as a sit skier in national competition but it was in the teens. There are only 2 to 3 other sit skiers on the team at any given time and none of them ever beat me. One incentive for keeping on winning at these national competitions was that we also won money for placing first. Eventually I reached "A" team designation. At this level all of our expenses were covered plus we received lots of gear; numerous pairs of free skis, poles, uniforms, sunglasses, hats and caps, gloves, boots and food all started to pile up. Also, my notoriety as an elite athlete began to grow.

We also were required to race in able-bodied ski races wherever we could across the country. I was back to racing just about every weekend. In a classic ski race on relatively flat terrain with the right conditions I was as competitive as any other standup classic skier. The press picked up quickly on the fact that someone sitting down was beating many of those that were standing up.

The American Birkebeiner, held annually in Hayward Wisconsin, was billed as the toughest Nordic ski race in North America. With a distance exceeding 50 kilometers it was challenge for anyone to accomplish. A typical year saw over five thousand leave the starting line. Before my injury, I had done the "Birke" ten times. A companion event called the Korteloppet was about half the distance. No one had ever skied either course sitting down. In 1991, I sit skied the "Korte". Then, in 1993 I finished the grueling Birke and beat over half of the competitors. People would ask in amazement how I managed to get up all of the steep hills. I would tell them that the up hills did not bother me; it was the screaming down hills that had me terrified.

One thing I enjoyed at West Yellowstone was the fact that we had Thanksgiving Day off. One of my favorite things was to ski into Yellowstone National Park on an un-plowed road that had a thick layer of snow on it. In the summer this road is jam packed with tourist in their automobiles. Now the road was closed to motorized traffic until the first of the year at which time snowmobiles and snow coaches were allowed. It was like having the entire Yellowstone National Park all to myself. I have great memories of skiing down this road and passing buffalo, elk and pausing to watch Bald Eagles on the Madison River. Little did I realize that in my later years my fondest memories of ski camp were those Thanksgiving Day solo skis into Yellowstone.

Chapter 11 - Skiing Golden in France

The 1992 Winter Olympics were held in France. Two weeks after the regular able-bodied Olympics the Paralympics were held. Since you might be wondering why the Olympics and Paralympics were not held at the same time there is a decent answer. It is because there would be too many people on the venues racing at the same time. The population of both the able and disabled winter Olympics is about equal. Now, I am the first one to admit that holding the Olympics and Paralympics all at the same time would be neat but it would be a logistical nightmare. So, I can understand why they are separated.

The downhill portion of the Paralympics was held in Albertville France. And that is where we stayed for the 10 days that we were in France. The cross-country venues were about 10 miles away near a small town called Tinges.

We flew from the USA to the City of Leon France which is about 4 hours by bus from the Olympic venues. We stayed in Leon overnight and had a chance to relax in the downtown part of the city. It was a warm spring evening and we did not even have jackets on.

I thought New York City cab drivers were crazy but they drive like a little old ladies compared to the drivers in this city in France. I don't know how we survived nor did I know if all the pedestrians in our way survived. It was one hell of a ride.

I don't think that the waiter in the restaurant that we ate dinner in liked Americans. Unbeknownst to me I ordered "steak tartar". I did not realize what I had ordered until they set it in from me. Steak tartar was a raw slab of hamburger with a raw egg with yolk starting to slide off to the side of the meat. The food did come with a side order of yes, you guessed it, French fries. I just ate the French fries but did not touch the nasty looking hamburger. But all was not lost, Jane ate it!

The only other foods I liked in France were the French pastries and the breads. I ate lot of bread.

I didn't have a clue about my competition and I don't have a lot of memories of the race and for that I get to blame Jane. We brought a camcorder along for her to film my competition. But in her excitement she turned the machine off when she thought she was filming me and turned the machine on with she thought she was not filming me. We have some amazing shots of Jane's feet!

The first race was two laps around the course with a couple of not very steep hills. Dual tracks were set that the racers were expected to ski in. But you did not have to stay in the tracks. It was legal to ski just outside of the tracks in what was called the skating lane. A strategy that I learned was that on some days the skating lane was fast and some days the tracks were faster. In fact some days the speed would vary on the racecourse depending on if you were in the shade or not. I skied a fair amount of that race in the skating lane.

Winning the race was a big surprise to me and I was quite ecstatic until…the Swiss National ski team petitioned the authorities stating that I was not disabled enough to be in the category that I was in and I should be disqualified from winning the gold medal. A Swiss skier had taken fourth place and could win a medal if they bounced me out of the first position.

That began several hours of uncertainty as a group of doctors from different countries consulted with each other and examined me in great detail. I had to undergo a lot of physical dexterity tests while a lot of people watched. The doctors then went into another room to discuss my case as we all waited in tense anticipation. After awhile they came out and announced that not only was I qualified I was more disabled than the criteria required. It was certified that I could never again have my disability questioned as long as I was at the world-class skiing level. The gold medal was mine!

One thing that bothers me to this day was the medal awards ceremony. The French said because they did not want to exploit the differences between countries they were not going to play the national anthem of the gold medal winning skier. Instead they played some blasé instrumental each time a medal was hung around a winner's neck. That was pretty disappointing.

After the first race I got sicker than a dog with the cold of a lifetime. I just stayed in my room and drank fluids and tried to sleep. All the French really had available was orange juice, Coca-Cola and red wine. I left the wine alone but drowned myself in orange juice and Coca-Cola.

My second race 3 days later was half the distance of the first race at 3.1 miles. It was one very fast lap around the entire course. I now had a bull's eye on my back as skiers knew who they had to beat. I had a good race until I was about 200 yards from the finish line. I came upon a Russian skier going relatively slow in the track that I was in. He was such a poor skier that he could not get out of the track like he was supposed to, allowing me to pass. When I reached him he was about ¾ out of the way but the tail end of his sit ski was still in my way. At that particular point on the track I was also unable to jump clear of him so I smacked him a glancing blow that sent him spinning into a snow bank and me on my way to a second gold medal. I was the only American skier able or disabled who won a cross-country medal that year in France. And no, the team psychiatrist was no longer employed by the ski team. I never saw him again after he let me out of the car in Bozeman Montana four years earlier.

Chapter 12 - Silver is Junk

The next winter Olympics were only two years in the future from 1992. The organizers of the summer and winter Olympics wanted to get on a schedule that had an Olympic event occurring somewhere in the world every two years instead of two events every four years. Thus, the summer or winter event had to be done two years earlier in order to get in the proper rotation. Because of this, many winter athletes who were approaching retirement decided to hang on and train for another two years. I was one of them.

The 1994 Winter Olympics were held in Lillehammer Norway. This time I would be racing three distances plus a fourth race which was a relay race with three other teammates. I was training hard but about a month before the race I felt an aching in my left shoulder that kept getting more and more painful as the Olympics approached.

We had been in Norway the year before in a warm up Olympic the event. We spent time in Beito attending the Ridderren after the pre Olympic warm up races in Lillehammer. It was another three weeks in my second favorite country. In the Lillehammer warm up races I took first every time and now I really had a bull's eye target on my back. Everyone was out to get me.

I hardly remember much about skiing in France. It was like I was a robot on automatic control. I vowed to myself that when I was in Norway for the Paralympics I would try to become much more of a human being. I planned to go into the Olympic Village more often and visit with people from other countries. I sort of let down my guard. And my sore shoulder was not helping my race times.

Prior to my first race it looked like I was going to have to withdraw because the shoulder pain was so bad. The national team Physician talked to the Paralympic authorities and received clearance to give me a steroid shot in the shoulder. I was nervous about the injection because I don't like needles but I was desperate. The shot was amazing and the pain in my shoulder disappeared and did not return for months afterwards.

In the first race I won the first Olympic silver medal of my career. I lost to a skier from France by about 5 seconds. In my second race I won the second Olympic silver medal of my career. I lost to the same skier from France this time by about 6 seconds. In my third race I won the third Olympic silver medal of my career. I lost to the same skier from France this time by about 3 seconds. What hurt more than losing three gold medals by less than 15 seconds was the fact that I had to sit on the awards stand and listen to the French national anthem three times. The Norwegian Olympic Committee discontinued the practice that was done in France regarding not playing the national anthem for the gold winning athlete. It took almost 13 years for me to get another crack at that Frenchman but I did. I'll tell you about that later in this book.

Winning is everything when you're at the world class level. I felt that I had let people down and maybe more regrettably my coaches felt that I'd let them down. The fact that I had now owned five of the seven Olympic medals won by USA Nordic skiers did not seem to carry any weight with the ski team coaches and administrators. (In the Norwegian Olympics I had won three medals, the able-bodied team did not win any medals and blind skier Michelle Drolet won the only woman's Nordic medal, bronze, ever in the 10 kilometer race. (Back in the 1970s U.S. able-bodied skier Bill Koch captured the first and only able-bodied ski medal, silver.)

After the completion of the Paralympics in Lillehammer the ski team boarded a bus back to Beito for the annual Ridderren event. At this point in time the national disabled ski team of Norway did not attend the Ridderren so most of the U.S. ski team athletes took home most of the medals. After that year, there was never another Ridderren event where the national Norwegian team was not in attendance. They would never again let that slaughter occur on their home turf. As far as I know the U.S. National ski team has never gone back to Beitostolen. But I did several times.

The Ridderren in one respect was like Ski for Light in that there were a lot of other things to do besides ski. The food was fantastic and every night there was a dance with a live band. There was a talent night and other social events. One night we even had the King and Queen of Norway award the medals for the day.

One thing the Americans did which was kind of goofy was to decorate wooden clothespins and hang them on unsuspecting people. Printed on the clothespin was a little note saying "Hello From the USA". Most people thought that they were a nice gesture and considered them souvenirs.

For instance I was standing behind the honor guard as the King of Norway was paraded in. Each soldier was standing at attention with their hands clasped behind their backs. I subtly placed the clothespin on the cuff of a soldier standing right in from me. When the king paraded by each soldier snapped to attention and saluted. When the poor guy in front of me saluted a bright red clothespin was sticking out from his arm. LOL!

Another night I was getting a medal on stage. A very pretty navy lieutenant was pinning the medals on our chests and giving us each a traditional hug. As the lady was giving me a hug I clipped the back of her collar with a clothespin. The audience responded with a larger than normal applause. The navy lieutenant had no clue until she got back in her group of what happened.

While the snow was fairly fast in Lillehammer it was blazing fast in Beito. In general, new fallen snow is slow snow because of its crystalline sharp structure. Snow that has been on the ground for awhile is faster because the crystalline structures have rounded off into ball shapes. This microscopic change really speeds up the glide on a pair of skis.

It had not snowed in Beitostolen for quite awhile making the snow really fast. It was there I raced my fastest 10 kilometer race ever. I went around the 6.2 mile course in just about 26 minutes flat. That means I was averaging about 1 mile every 4 ½ minutes and that is very fast for any skier standing or sitting.

Mark Wellman was another paraplegic on the U.S. ski team that I was friends with. You'll read a lot more about Mark in the next chapter of this book. Here in Beitostolen, Mark was looking for someone to guide him in the 10K race. A brash young U.S. army sergeant was talked into doing the race with Mark. Before the race the young man was talking smack. He sort of was condescending and thought he would have no problem keeping up with a disabled skier. When the gun went off for Mark to start he left the smart talking Sergeant in his dust. The guy never caught Mark.

At the banquet that night I happen to run into the sergeant. To his credit, he had put aside his own embarrassments and was very complimentary of Mark. The sergeant mentioned that Mark had skied the 10 kilometers in about 28 minutes which was certainly the fastest time of the day. As the beaming sergeant was turning to leave he said to me, "By the way how did you do today"? When I mentioned that I skied the race faster than Mark by over 2 minutes he just about dropped his teeth!

As I mentioned earlier, it is common for royalty from Norway to attend these kinds of events; the Olympics, Paralympics and the Ridderren. On our last day, a bright cloudless day, in Beito Jane and I went outside to take a walk. Just as we did, a black limousine pulled up next to the door and a bunch of King's Guards jumped out and one opened the door for who amazingly was Harald, the King of Norway. Soon to follow him out of the car was his wife, Sonia, the Queen.

He motioned for Jane and I to come over and talk. We must have spent at least ten minutes talking to him about the USA, skiing and how we did in the Paralympics. At one point I pulled out a clothespin. I asked if I could pin him figuring I wouldn't get away with it if I tried to do it when he turned his back. He said of course. When I reached for him to make the pin on his Norwegian sweater all the guards went for their guns thinking that I was attacking their royal highness. The King quickly raised his hands motioning to the guards to drop their weapons. The King had a little bit of a beer belly and I pinned him right in the front. The Queen and Jane both had quite a chuckle. The guards remained stoic. But the ten minutes with the king and queen of Norway was one of the most amazing meetings that I can tell you about in this book.

When we got back to United States the entire Olympic and Paralympics teams were invited to the White House for several days. We had audiences with President Bill Clinton, Vice President Al Gore and their wives. We signed wooden Easter eggs for the upcoming Easter egg roll on the White House lawn. We also had a reception at the Hard Rock Café and saw a play at the Ford Theater where Abraham Lincoln was assassinated by John Wilkes Booth. We toured various Washington monuments. We also paired off with Olympic able bodied athletes and were taken to local schools in the Washington area where we spoke again about our disabilities and our experiences at the Paralympic and Olympic events.

As we were signing Easter eggs on the first floor of the White House I felt the call of nature so I needed to find a bathroom. A secret service agent was summoned and escorted me to an elevator where we went downstairs to the basement of the White House. He then directed me to a bathroom that was huge. He opened the door and clicked on the lights. I went in and he shut the door and I did my business.

I noticed that the paper towels near the sink one used to dry hands had the presidential seal on them so I took a few for souvenirs. When I came out into the hallway there was no one to be found. I was not sure quite how to get back to the elevator. Finally I found a room with a door ajar and I thought I would stick my head and get directions. It turned out to be the nerve center of the secret service. They seemed to have a fit when I came through the door. I was quickly escorted out of the room and back to the elevator and up to the first floor, and that was my private tour of the White House!

Here is my reason why I think Bill Clinton was elected president twice. Up front and personal he certainly is a people person. The president's mother had died of cancer just a few weeks earlier. One of my main ski team sponsors was the JanSport Corporation. I mentioned earlier, that among other things they printed logos on shirts. They printed up two special sweat shirts for the Clintons regarding fighting breast cancer for me to give to them.

When I was my turn to meet them in the receiving line I handed the two sweatshirts to Mr. Clinton and his wife Hillary. Mrs. Clinton was particularly excited and expressed hope that there were two of them and that they would fit. I had my picture taken with them as well with Tipper and Al Gore.

That night there was a $1,000 a plate fundraising banquet at the White House. Before the dinner the Olympic teams were on the stage in bleachers. The wheelchair users were situated in the front row. We're very close to the podium where the speakers would talk. After the President gave his remarks he turned around and started walking off the stage where he started shaking hands with each wheelchair user in the front row. When he got to me, he took my hand and shook it and looked me in the eyes and said, "Jeff, Hillary and I thank you again for the shirts you gave us today and we will wear them". I was amazed that here was a guy that had met over 200 athletes that afternoon and then probably attended to several world problems and yet he still had the presence of mind to remember my name and the shirts I've given them. I was impressed!

Chapter 13 - Sking in Japan - Ski for Light the Later Years

By fall, 1994, at the age of 46, I pretty much had retired from racing for the U.S. team, but felt I still had something to contribute. I liked to work out and felt I was in pretty good shape. Also, my shoulder felt fine.

I was sort of like other professional athletes in that I did not really know when to retire and changed my mind a couple of times.

I happened to be in Colorado on a consulting job and I touched base with one of the ski team coaches John Kreammelmeyer. J. K. lived in Frisco Colorado not far from a beautiful blacktopped bike trail. One morning we went out for run, he was actually running and I was double polling in my wheelchair. I think it was a test of the coaches to see if I still had what it took to be on the ski team. I learned later J. K. reported that he was surprised at what good a shape I was in, and that my sore shoulder did not seem to be a problem.

At some point that summer I asked the coaching staff if I could come back and help coach sit skiers. They not only told me no they told me no with a nasty vengeance. The head coach, Kendall Butts was quoted as saying, "All Pagels wants is a team uniform". His comments not only irritated me, it made me feel very sad.

That winter the U.S. National Championships were going to be held in Cable Wisconsin. Cable was about 5 hours from where we lived in Green Bay. The disabled team would be there competing like they do every year at the national cross country ski championships. By this time there were three other sit skiers trying to make the "A" team. None of them had ever beat me and none of them had ever won an Olympic medal.

I drove to Cable to meet the team and to race just as a citizen at the race. For the one night I was in Cable I stayed in a rental cabin with the rest of the team. I could sense the hostility to me by the team coaches. It was palatable. The talk was small and helped me to make up my mind that my ski team days were truly over. I decided to stay for next day's race and then I would leave.

Early the next morning the coaches used their waxing expertise to attempt to make the sit skiers skis extremely fast. I did my own waxing.

I did not know what to expect before the race. I did not give myself an absolute chance of winning the race as a couple of the skiers had been skiing hard and were in excellent shape. I certainly was not in world-class physical shape that winter. The five-kilometer course was very technical with lots of hills both up and down. To make a fast race story short, I beat everyone. And as I recall I won by quite a bit. I picked up my last U.S. ski team medal and headed for my van and I never looked back.

I do remember the drive home from Cable. I remember stopping for gas and using the pay phone at the gas station to call home to Jane. I told her about the race and that my ski team career was over. I felt a sense of calmness. On the way home I did something that I and others in my circle of jocks are prone to do once we accomplish something good. Disgustingly, we stop at a Kentucky Fried Chicken and down a greasy meal of finger licking chicken. Yum, yum.

Around December of 1994 I received a telegram. I had never received a telegram before. This one was from the country of Japan. It was the coach of the Japanese national disabled cross country ski team inviting me to Japan for two weeks to advise their coaching staff and a group of disabled skiers. Japan was a country I had never visited. The Japanese would pay all my expenses. I would be working alongside another foreign disabled sit skier, Harald, a man from Norway. He and I became fast friends and kept in touch over the years until he passed away from cancer in 2009.

The flight over to Japan was fine. I remember taking off from Austin Strauble Field in Green Bay as the National Football League's Green Bay Packers were playing a championship game at Lambeau Field. As usual, the stadium was packed, but the streets of Green Bay were deserted. It was a short flight to Minneapolis where I had to wait about three hours to board my airplane for the long but direct flight to Japan. I passed some of the time in the airport bar watching the tail end of the Packers game.

I left Green Bay on a Sunday, but because I crossed the International Date Line, I landed in Japan on a Monday even though it was still Sunday night in Green Bay. I was met at the Airport in Narita Japan by my hosts for the two weeks I would be there. I've never met such a kind and gracious of people as the Japanese.

I spent the first night in Tokyo at a disabled hostel. It was like half rehabilitation center and half hotel. I could certainly get used to some of their traditions. Each floor of the complex had a Japanese bath that you signed up for 1 hour each evening. Gosh, that really felt good as I've always liked hot, hot water. Harald, also staying on my floor, came out of the bath wrapped in a towel and said in broken English, "Jeff look at my feets they look like shrimps". To this day Jane and I call our feet feets and shrimp shrimps. And we both fondly think of Harold when we purposely miss-state those words.

After breakfast the next morning I rolled outside to have a look around. On a nearby park bench sat an elderly lady. Above her in a tree perched a crow cawing noisily. I said to the lady that the crow was cawing in English. She commented that if all countries spoke the same language like crows we would not have dropped the atomic bomb on them. I had no retort for that comment and silently moved on.

We left the next day by train for the small community of Nagano Japan. It took almost an entire day of traveling to get there. I didn't mind as it was fascinating looking out of the windows as the world of Japan passed us by. I saw lots of farmland, rice fields, cities, and mountains. The hotel we stayed in Nagano was where the entire ski team stayed. I really enjoyed the Japanese cuisine. Much of the food was raw or boiled. I never once got sick and still eat Japanese food whenever I have the opportunity.

The Japanese of course had TV and the most popular show by far was sumo wrestling. Apparently it was a time of the year for the national sumo championships to be played out. However on the second Sunday in Japan I watched the Packers play on Japanese television. It took exactly 1 hour to watch the game as all that was shown was each play. There were no commercials, no replays, and no huddles. The only thing they showed was the actual minutes and seconds when there was action. That was one interesting way to watch a professional football game!

Harald and I stayed in Nagano about eight days skiing every day and showing the Japanese all we knew about sit skiing. It was fun and it was rewarding. We had them do all sorts of training exercises. Some of the disabled skiers were brand new and didn't have very much expertise when it came to sit skiing. I took several them to the base of the hill. I had them climb the hill just a few yards and turn around and slide down. Most of them made it down in one piece. Then I had them climb the hill a few more yards, but by the end of several hours the entire group was bombing the hill with newfound expertise.

I also had the skiers ski single file behind each other. The last skier in the queue was to jump out of the track and ski as fast as he could to the front of the line where he would jump back inside the tracks and set the pace. Then the last skier in the queue would replicate what the first skier had done. This was a cardiovascular challenge to these skiers but they performed very well. By the end of the eight days Harald and I were calling them our skiers and not somebody else's.

I also had a chance to ski all the Olympic and Paralympics ski courses. I had a chance to check out the elevations and dangerous corners. I also was given maps of the trails. Those I brought back to the USA.

At the end of eight days we were driven by automobile back to Tokyo. There we spent the next few days touring this great city and eating fantastic food. The beer was pretty tasty too!

The flight back to Green Bay was interesting in one respect. Actually, I landed back in Green Bay before I even left Japan! It was that International Date Line paying me back for the day I lost on the way over.

Even during the Olympic years I faithfully attended Ski for Light every winter someplace in the country. By then the mobility impaired program was a well oiled machine with lots of support and lots of interest. I was also on the Ski for Light planning committee every year which resulted in me going to the event cities every fall to lay the groundwork for that winters event.

Ski for Light was truly an international event with a large contingent of skiers from Norway and also some from England, France, Canada and even Japan. In 1997, at the end of the event in Granby Colorado the Japanese contingent came to the SFL board and asked us to send four skiers to Japan to help form the Japanese version of Ski for Light. I was one of the skiers selected to go to Japan. I could not believe my good fortune returning to the country where I had been to just three years earlier. Instead of training elite skiers this time I would be training basic rookie level disabled people in the sport of cross country skiing.

This trip unfolded much like the last time. I was in Japan with gracious hosts greeting me at the Airport and taking care of every want and need. I was able to have a reunion with some of my disabled ski team friends from my last trip as well as make many new ones.

One unique difference between Ski for Light Japan and the USA version of Ski for Light was this. In Japan it was a family affair. The disabled skier would bring wives, husbands, sons and daughters or grandparents to the event. In the early evening after the dinner hour there would be recreational activities for the entire family. However, later in the evening the adults would get together for the tremendous consumption of alcoholic beverages into the early hours of the day. This is truly a trip where once again I had to sleep on the plane ride home!

Chapter 14 - Skiing Over the Sierra Mountain Range

In 1993, at the age of 45, I and another U.S. Disabled Ski Team member, Mark Wellman successfully completed a 50-mile cross-country ski trek. Now, 50 miles is tough enough, but this ski was across the Sierra Nevada mountain range in eastern California near Yosemite National Park. While we did have a camera/video crew along, the plan was that they do nothing to help us. We wanted to do this trip on our own. Mark was a big wall paraplegic mountain climber who was famous for some dangerous climbs all over the world. However, for this adventure, he felt he needed a partner, so he asked me.

We encountered 50-mph winds, 50^0 temperature swings, avalanches, extreme sunburn and deep snow. But we also saw stupendous scenery and gained a better understanding of the existing technology that can allow wheelchair users the freedom to access the wilderness. We also gained a heightened awareness of self-reliance and a natural high that was the reward for pushing our bodies to the limits and succeeding. Here in diary form are my recollections of that adventure.

DAY ONE

Today is Saturday, April 10, 1993 and it is just getting light. Outside of our motel room in the small town of Lee Vining, California the birds are singing, the sky is clear blue and the temperature is a balmy 50^0F. We had planned to start our trip the day before but 70 mph winds near the top of the mountain range even scared seemingly foolish risk takers like Mark and me into waiting an extra day.

As we rechecked and packed our gear in the van waiting to take us to the start, we both tried to again lighten our 40-plus-lb pulks (sleds) that we intended to pull behind our sit skis. Once we started out, there would be no second chance to retrieve anything sorely needed, but again we did not want to carry something we were not going to use. We packed lots of food including deer sausage and cheese from Wisconsin, drinking water, sleeping bags, bivy sacks, cooking and first aid kits, rope, ice axes, extra ski poles and baskets. We also took a little extra clothing like hats, mittens and gloves. We did not take tents as we planned to sleep right in the snow banks. If you have ever tried to erect a tent, you know why we did not bring a tent!

On the three-mile ride up the snow free Tioga Pass to Ellery Lake, the weather began to deteriorate. At the snow-line, the winds were exceeding 50 mph, and the estimated wind chill was 30^0F below zero. However, we had come too far to delay the trip again, so with hugs to family members, off we went. Just before we left, my son, Chad pointed across the frozen lake to a lone coyote trotting along glancing our way. What in the world was that critter doing up here near the tree line?

Within the first 500 yards of the start we encountered a severe side slope. This is a condition in which the snow drifts across the trail at about a 45^0 angle. It required us to lean heavily uphill, use an ice axe to keep from sliding down the slope, and use only one arm to propel with both ski poles on the downhill side. The 40-pound pulks we towed behind us were unmercifully obeying the law of gravity and trying hard to pull us down the hundred feet or so of drop off.

Because we were so close to the start, Jane and the boys watched in fear and growing concern. (She was not too thrilled about this entire project to start with!) I was not exactly happy with the situation myself. I thought I could not possibly go 50 miles like this. Mark on the other hand was doing well with this first dilemma. He had years of experience in the western mountains both as an able-bodied and disabled climber. He also had metal edged skis that cut a firm purchase in the snow. I had racing skis that did not do that and I had quite a battle on my hands.

After the first half mile however, the trail flattened out and the going got a lot easier. Within an hour we were in a groove and making good time. To help, the wind died down and the sun came out. At the time this seemed like a blessing, but little did I know that I was in store for the worst case of sunburn in my life.

We were taking the occasional side slopes in stride and enjoying the scenery when it became apparent that the snow was softening due to the warming temperatures. Our racing ski pole baskets were sinking deeper and deeper as were our ski frames themselves. Even after we changed to our mountain ski poles with wider baskets our progress became slower and slower. After seven hours of skiing, we were getting tired and still had about two miles to go to reach our first nights objective at Tuolumne Meadows.

Just before the sun set over the mountains we reached the meadow and started to set up our camp. "Camp" is not really a good word to define our setup which consisted of digging out a shallow "grave', unrolling a bivy sack and bag and crawling in. It was getting cold, and as soon as the sun went down, all of our gear became coated with heavy frost.

Both Mark and I were big eaters, so we packed a bunch of food. However, except for being a little thirsty, we were not hungry and we stayed that way almost for the entire trip. (Experts told us later that a combination of stress and altitude shut down our desire to eat.)

Knowing I should eat something, I fired up the small camp stove and cooked up some freeze-dried beef and rice. It tasted great, but I was just not hungry. When I asked Mark if he wanted some, he responded with a snore!

Since I am paralyzed from the waist down, it was no easy task crawling into the sleeping bag in deep snow. I ended up with about a hat full of the unwelcome white stuff with me every time I got into the bag. During the three nights we slept out on the trail, I never did master getting in, without dragging some snow along. The excellent clothing I wore saved me from miserable nights. Eventually the snow melted, my legs stayed warm and I drifted off, looking at a zillion stars that seemed just out of arms reach.

DAY TWO

Easter Sunday broke without any wind or a cloud in the sky. One of our photographers said his thermometer registered 12^0 above zero. The soft snow of yesterday afternoon turned rock hard as did the remains of my beef stew. I had to use my ice axe to chip out the spoon from the frozen kettle.

Since it looked as though the day would warm quickly, we hurriedly packed and set off. The icy snow was a lot easier to ski on, despite the fact that we were stiff, sore and had badly burned faces. Despite the heavy application of high quality sunscreen even the inside of my nose and ears were burned from the close reflection off the snow. Our lips were swollen and the skin was coming off in shreds. Breakfast was never considered and we had enough water to wait another day before having to find or make more.

The day moved by uneventfully, (if one can call skiing in the pristine solitude of the Sierra Nevada mountain range "uneventful"), until the early afternoon when we encountered our first avalanche. It became apparent that we could not ski the side slope along the face of the avalanche, because it looked like more snow and rocks could give way at any moment.

Our alternative was to descend about 75 yards into the trees off the trail and try to make our way through the forest below the avalanche until we could hook back up with the trail. Mark, the ever daring one, elected to ski down a headwall and take his chances missing the giant Sequoia trees. With special spikes attached to his ski poles, he was successful and made it to the bottom safe and dry.

My experience, however, was another story. I elected to dismount, rope my ski and pulk together, drop them down the headwall and then slide down on my rear end. It worked all right, except for getting fairly soaked from the wet snow. The large trees in the woods also presented another problem. The warm spring sun reflecting off the tree trunks created huge sinkholes around every tree. We had to skirt from spot to spot trying to avoid being sucked into one of hundreds of holes. Eventually we found our way out of the woods and set across a mile of frozen Tenaya Lake. Because of our experience the day before, we wanted to quit earlier, dry out our sleeping bags, melt a fresh supply of water and recover some strength. It was not to be.

At the end of Tenaya Lake, the bright sunshine had melted the snow enough that it was impossible to ski up the steep bank leading back to the trail. Using both of our ice axes, I was able to butt myself up the bank using the axes like snowshoes. Once on top of the hill, I pulled both pulks and Mark up the hill to wear we could start skiing on the trail again.

With about three hours of daylight remaining, we moved out quickly as our camp was only about a mile up the trail. With less than a quarter mile to our destination, Olmstead Point, we skied smack into another avalanche. This time there was no opportunity to ski down and around. "Down" was more than 1,000 feet down and if we did make it down, we had no idea if we would ever make it up again. Mark led the assault, inching his way along the steep side slope. For once the soft snow became an asset, allowing him to set a track with his metal edged skis and keep the pulk in line. About 20 yards from safety the trail turned upward, and in an instant, Mark lost his grip and started plummeting down the slope. Instinctively he plunged his ice ax into the mushy snow and preformed a classic self-rescue stop after only 20 yards or so of free falling. Using the butting technique we learned on Tenaya Lake he somehow made it back to safety on the trail.

Now it was decision time for me. I had been skiing for nine hours and was wet, cold and getting very nervous. I thought of my family, lifestyle and all that was dear to me and decided to ask for help. One of the photographers along on the trip was nearby and I swallowed my pride and asked him to position himself down slope from me and check my progress with the side of his body. With his help, I quickly accomplished the traverse and was on the other side with Mark. Mark was ecstatic that he made the crossing un-assisted and I was very happy I made it across anyway I could to enjoy another day.

With a half hour before dark, we hurriedly made sleeping preparations and jumped inside our bags before the evening frost covered everything. That night, the stars seemed even closer…I could almost reach them.

DAY THREE

This was to be our long mile day. We had only come about 15 miles in two days and still had 35 to go. From our maps and Mark's previous trips to the area, he felt the worst terrain and avalanches were over. There were going to be some hard miles and technical climbs. I could handle "hard"; I was just getting a little gun shy of technical.

The stars were still out and the sun just a promise in the eastern sky when we lifted ourselves into the sit skis and started out again on frozen snow. In about 20 minutes our stiff and sore muscles loosened up and progress was pretty fast. Most of the day consisted of long downhill runs followed by not so long up hills. One of the best parts of the trip occurred on this day, when

I skied downhill continuously for more than an hour on a gentle descent. I felt like the Santa Claus in the Norelco Shaver commercial on TV! When I was leading, the only marks on the snow were from occasional wandering bears that were just starting to come out of hibernation.

About noon, I came across a granite rock wall that had a stream of snow-melt running down like a mini waterfall. I was able to just reach out with my empty water bottle and fill it up. That water tasted good and actually made me a bit hungry. Here, I need to digress a little bit and tell you my sardine story.

Earlier that winter, I was at a Ski for Light event in South Dakota. As is customary, on Friday night a traditional Norwegian meal was served complete with canned sardines as an appetizer. Hoarder that I am, I kept some un-opened cans in my backpack. That backpack accompanied me to the Pre-Paralympic games in Lillehammer, Norway where I did not eat them. But, now I had that same pack along and still had the cans of sardines. So, here near the top of the Sierra Nevada about a year later, I opened the tins and enjoyed those fish and the fresh snowmelt. It was a lunch I still remember to this day!

According to the map, we only had one more mile to go to our next campsite. Maybe for once we could get there early, dry some gear out, and relax. Not!

After having come more than 24 miles from daybreak with no major surprises, we came upon a fresh avalanche that must have occurred only hours before. Uprooted trees and big rocks lying on top of the snow made the 100-yard crossing downright ominous. We looked around and realized that at any moment more snow could come over the steep ledge on which we were perched.

Whispering quietly, we planned our escape. First, we tried to ski up the side of the avalanche, but the soft snow made pole planting impossible. So, plop off the sit ski I went again and began butting my way across the avalanche. Mark did the same this time as there was no way I could pull him through the debris. We spent about two hours butting and crawling the 100 yards of slidden snow and tree branches. One thing I still remember was the very pungent smell of evergreen from the broken trees. Funny how years later, only the positive memory stuck with me.

Finally, we both made it across, breathed a sigh of relief, remounted our sit skis and poled the remaining half mile to our final evening campsite next to a raging waterfall. We had an hour before dark, and the sun helped us partially dry our gear. In celebration, we cooked up a meal of burrito stew followed by chocolate chip cookies. Even with depressed appetites, this was pretty good stuff. Going to sleep one last time under the stars, I was sure we were going to make it and wanted this adventure to be over. My gas tank was about empty. Mark on the other hand was in his element. Somewhat sadly, he mused about the possibility of skiing back the way we came to avoid having his dream end.

DAY FOUR

We only had ten miles to go and had told our friends and family that we planned to appear at noon at the end of the trail at Crane Flats. We were so confident in our abilities; we slept in an hour after sunrise and slowly packed for our last day. For three miles, we skied uphill. Because we were back below the tree line, we encountered two places where large Sequoia trees had crashed across the trail. They proved to be only minor obstructions compared to the avalanches we had been through. The last seven miles were all downhill. We could tell we were dropping in elevation, the snow depths were decreasing and on south facing slopes, bare ground was visible.

A welcome sight appeared as I came around yet another corner. My oldest son, Corey was skiing up to us. After hugs and handshakes, we met Jane, son Chad and Mark's girlfriend all skiing up to see us. Mark and I continued to pull our own pulks but both Corey and Chad became Sherpas for the camera crew. Those guys were more than happy to get rid of some of their gear. We all skied down the remaining mile to a waiting group of media and other well-wishers. Champagne bottles were uncorked, pictures taken and stories retold. Mark was the tough guy and held up well under numerous questions from the press. One reporter asked me a tough question about being happy the trip was over and I broke down and cried like a baby. After what we went through, they were tears of relief and happiness.

There were showers to take, steaks to eat, and beers to toast, so we packed the van and headed to Yosemite Village. My last look up the trail was out the window of the van. I looked twice, unbelieving at first, and then understanding. There on the trail was a coyote, sitting with eyes fixed on me. When we made eye contact, it stood up, turned and trotted back up the trail. Folks ask me if we had help on the trip and I have to wonder if that coyote was not an expression of something more powerful than what we have on earth. Was that animal my guardian angel? I would like to think so.

Chapter 15 - Climbing Tahoma (Mt. Rainier)

In 1999, at the age of 49, we finally put the pieces of a puzzle together and figured out how to try climbing a mountain. The seeds were first planted after my 1993 ski across the Sierra Nevada mountain range, but it took six years of planning, thinking and fundraising to put in place an effort to do what no one else had done.

I had picked up a bunch of Outdoor Industry sponsors after my ski over the Tioga Pass and met a bunch of interesting outdoorsy people. One, Lou Whittaker from the State of Washington, suggested that I come out and climb Mt. Rainier. Lou was a renowned climber even then at 71 years of age and held the record for the most summits of Rainier. This mountain, at 14,400 feet in elevation is not the highest mountain in the USA, but it is considered the hardest to summit. Of the ten thousand people that try to get to the top every year, only about half of them make it. At that point, no wheelchair user had ever summited.

The main reason I wanted to try mountain climbing was because it would be a higher level of competition between me and myself. I did not have to beat anyone to achieve success. And, even if the mountain beat me, it was ok because I took the journey. At least that was what other climbers preached.

After the 1994 Olympics, I was asked to give a presentation on "How the Olympics Promote World Peace". I agreed to travel to a college in Marshall, Minnesota. They were holding a World Peace Conference. I had about a year to prepare a presentation. Well, a year flew by and I had a problem. After what I experienced at the two Paralympics and learned from others, there were no good examples of how these games promoted world peace. I ended up telling the audience to choose a person from each country and have them form a team to try to climb a mountain. That would promote world peace! I got a standing ovation.

At this point in my life I was asked to do quite a few epic adventures. One was to ski to the South Pole and get there in time to celebrate the new millennium. Another invitation came to ski across Greenland. Finding vacation time and finances limited my choices. Climbing mountains piqued my interest because it seemed to be something I could accomplish even if I lived in relatively flat Wisconsin and even if I had no real knowledge of how I could go about climbing.

In 1999, my friend and inventor Dave Stubenvol finally came up with a design that seemed workable. Dave used simple climbing technology, (ropes, stakes, carabineers and skis) which he named the Summiter.

The Summiter was a metal tube device that attached to the front of a sit ski. The climbing rope, (200 feet) was passed through two devices called jumars that either pinched the rope so I could pull up or released so I could reach ahead for another length of rope. It had three positions depending on how steep the pitch was. I could have pulled up an almost vertical wall about an inch at a time. On a 45^0 slope I could gain about a foot each time a pulled the bar toward me. I needed four team members to make the operation run smoothly. While I was climbing one pitch of rope, two of the team would be setting the next 200 feet. The plan was for the team to leapfrog up the mountain. This time, I used metal edged alpine skis and I had an extra pair mounted just a bit higher than the pair on which I was skiing. When the snow got warm, both sets of skis did the job of keeping me "afloat". My team members used snowshoes. Why 200 feet of climbing rope you might ask? Simple, that is the length of rope that team members could easily toss over their back and climb.

I was responsible for much of the pre-climb organizing. There were many details to work out. We or I should say, wooed sponsors for all sorts of gear including tents, sleeping gear, camp food and climbing rope. I also had to secure government permits as Mt. Rainier is a national park and everyone has to have a permit to climb. The feds were not too excited about our adventure and our relationship stayed rocky before, during and after the climb. I also had to coordinate schedules for 10 people, five of whom were professional guides. In fact, when just when it seemed our departure date was set for May 31, we had to delay the start to June 15 because lead guide Kurt Wedberg was leading a trip up Alaska's Mt. McKinley.

I also learned that another wheelchair user, Peter Rieke, was also trying to summit the mountain. He used an arm powered handcycle/snow machine that looked like a miniature bulldozer. He did not summit in 1998 and was going to try again at the same time I was making my attempt.

Besides attending to organizational matters, our team members from Wisconsin, Corey and Chad, friend Jim Wallen and of course, Dave Stubenvol spent some weekends simulating climbing mountains. We would go out on steep cross-country ski trails and practice going up one side and down the other. We set up our tents and took them down, always trying to do it faster and smarter. In addition, we kept modifying our gear to make it work better.

Endurance training was vitally important. In the Olympics I trained for speed, now I trained to do smaller amounts of work but for long, long periods. It was not about going very fast; it was just about going. I would go for three to four hour bike rides or kayak paddles. It was very enjoyable.

I took to occasionally sleeping on a cot on our home's outdoor deck in my sleeping bag and bivy sack. I was hoping it would toughen me up for what was to come on the mountain. Truth be known, I rarely slept well in temperatures below freezing.

As our start date came close, we garnered attention from the news media. A national news network, (Fox) local affiliate, (Channel 11) decided to send a crew along with us to document the adventure. The film they produced after the climb won many awards in media circles. More importantly, Connie Fellman, the TV personality who made the trip became fast friends with all of us and actually ended up making two more climbs with us in Norway and Africa.

Our first day on the mountain started both good and bad. My relationship with the National Park Service worsened. The building where the permit was to be picked up was not wheelchair accessible because there were about 20 steps between the entrance door and me. Rather than send one of my team to get the climbing permit, I elected to protest the steps by not getting the permit at all.

And, the rope we brought along turned out to be very stretchy and what we needed was a "static" rope that had very little stretch in it. Luckily, we talked our cameraman into driving almost two hours to Seattle to pick up more rope. We also borrowed some from Lou Whittaker.

On the bright side, we met our "expert" climber/guides that were to take us up the mountain. We took an instant liking to them and I think them to us. We spent the day working out details on how our apparatus worked and just how we were going to climb. I think they were impressed with Dave's contraption!

That night back at the Whittaker "bunkhouse" we did our final packing preparations and then hit the hay. Tomorrow we would start to climb.

There was a plethora of news media at our starting point as we strung the first pitch of rope. It was somewhat anticlimactic as I moved ever so slowly up the hill, but at least I was moving! One pitch followed the next and soon enough we were alone on the mountain moving up and up.

At about two hours into the climb, we hit a dense fog bank that limited visibility to less than 100 yards so our media team had to turn back. Their original plan was to go with us to our first campsite higher up the hill. About another two hours of climbing in the fog brought us above the cloud layer and into intense sunshine. And, it was warm. This was fun as everything was working as planned. An unexpected bonus was that the second pair of skis attached to my frame also kept me "floating" on the soft snow rather than sinking in as I did on the ski over the Trans-Sierra.

At one point, we were overtaken by a Park Service warden who warned us not to go over a certain part of the mountain because there were endangered grasses in that location. To change our course to miss 25 feet of terrain would have been a "big deal" for us, so after he left, we went through the endangered area anyway. I was carried the suspect 25 feet by team members who stepped from rock to rock thus not stepping on any visible vegetation.

As we set up our first camp and prepared supper, we were surprised to learn that the guide team was eating cold fried chicken and garden salads while we were swallowing freeze-dried something. A lesson we learned for future climbs was to try to bring fresh food instead of the blah stuff we had packed.

We reached the 10,000-foot mark at Camp Muir well before the second nightfall. Camp Muir was a popular location for climbers to bivouac before making a summit attempt. It was customary to awaken at midnight and start climbing in order to reach the summit at sunrise. However, when we arrived there were many disappointed climbers returning from NOT making the summit due to very high winds.

Nothing at Camp Muir, (bathrooms and a rudimentary bunkhouse) was wheelchair accessible. I guess park planners never figured someone using a wheelchair would ever get there so, why bother making the place accessible. I had a devil of a time getting into the bathroom, but managed with the help of my team to get in and then out. After I got home, I filed an American with Disabilities lawsuit against the Park Service for allowing an inaccessible building to be built at a public national park. That caused lots of controversy at all levels of government about how far to go to make things barrier free in the out of doors.

The third day brought more trouble as the warm weather and bright sunshine had melted what snow there was for the next 800 yards or so of mountain. What faced us was a rocky expanse of slope that rendered my Summiter rig useless. However, our guides saved the day. They fashioned out of climbing rope what was a huge frame that they used to backpack me on the back of the strongest of the guides who then carried me the 800 yards. Zack never took me off his back but rested every once in awhile against a boulder while the others carried all the rest of the gear over the rocky expanse.

Once we got back on snow cover, we were in a place called the Ingram Flats. It was not flat, but it certainly was not as steep as most of the mountain. We climbed and pulled our way across the flats to a point just below a prominence called "Disappointment Cleaver". The cleaver was infamous for life claiming ice and snow falls. It was the last treacherous spot we had to overcome before reaching the summit.

As we bedded down for our third night, some of the guides went ahead to check out conditions at the cleaver. The report they returned with was not good. Due to the warm weather the snow pack had become dangerously soft. The snow pickets that held my rope in place would not hold. So, at 11,100 feet my attempt to go higher was finished.

There is a mountaineering saying, "Summiting is optional, descending is mandatory". I could not agree more. While part of my brain was disappointed at not being able to try to go higher, most of my brain had had enough and was ready to go back down.

So, on the fourth day we started our descent down Rainier. What took us three days to go up took only part of one day to go down. Except for another carry over the snowless drop just above Camp Muir the rest of the descent was like a dog sled in reverse. Each of the five guides had a rope to me who would lead the way. With ski poles and gravity we almost ran down the mountain. It was fun and fast.

This was a new experience for me in that while not making it to the top, the adventure was still successful and still brings back many fond memories.

I want to finish this chapter by mentioning our fascination with First Nation or Indian culture. The entire team embraced the notion that the great outdoors is in one way a Church. It was a place to be respected, undamaged and embraced with reverence. We learned that the tops of mountains were sacred places for Natives of those areas. In fact, many climbers do not go to the ultimate top of a mountain as to not bother the Deities that reside there. We all took First Nation names and still use them to this day. I am Rainbow for the Happy and Sad occurrences in my life. Corey was Flying Fish because of his love of Swimming, Chad was Charging Spirit from a nickname we gave him when he was young. Jim was Soaring Bird and Dave was Ten Beers for his love of the amber nectar. Connie was Storyteller and our Cameraman was Eagle Eye.

The names of mountains usually come from those that discovered them when white men first visited. Mt. Rainier is named for a surveyor on a ship who saw the mountain from the Pacific Ocean. The First Nation name for the Mountain is Tahoma. We prefer to use the Indian names.

Chapter 16 - Climbing Mt. Galdopiggen in Norway

William O. Douglas was credited with saying that "the struggle of man against man produces jealousy, deceit, frustration, bitterness and hate. But, the struggle of man against the mountains is different. Man then bows before something that is bigger than he. And, when he does that, he finds serenity, humility and dignity."

I certainly believed in that quote and experienced exactly what Douglas was talking about in the Paralympics and other world-class competitions. This mountain climbing stuff was indeed strong medicine for what ailed me both physically and mentally.

In the spring of 1999, I was in the middle of planning and training for our attempt to summit Tahoma or Mt. Rainier. However, I also made a ninth trip to Norway to ski in the annual Ridderren events held in Beito. I used this trip to put in place plans to return in the summer of 2000 to climb Mt Galdopiggen. At 8,100 feet, it is the tallest summit in Northern Europe. The first climber to reach the top of this "spike" did so in 1850. Now, 150 years later, wheelchair users were about to try to get to the top as well.

I learned as much as I could about Galdopiggen and the logistics we had to put in place for the climb. It appeared that the adventure was doable. Our plan called for two of us to pull ourselves up the mountain using Summiters and bring five blind climbers along to experience the thrill of getting to high altitudes. In addition to my regular climb team, we brought along our wives, Connie Fellman - our journalist from the Tahoma Climb, and Wendy Martin - an executive with Polarmax, one of our clothing sponsors.

We choose July of 2000 to climb. There would still be plenty of snow on the mountain but the weather promised to be fairly warm and benign. It should also be noted that while I was in Norway, Peter Rieke was finally successful in summiting Mt. Rainier. I am glad he finally made it to the top of that hill!

Sture Bjorkness was a friend from the Norwegian city, Trondheim who also was a paraplegic caused by a car accident. He was about my age and while not as crazy about climbing, was a gamer and willing to try to become the first Norwegian wheelchair user to summit Galdopiggen.

My key Norwegian contact was Svein Thorestensen from Oslo. Svein did all of the coordinating on that side of the Atlantic from getting climbing permits to reserving hotel rooms as well as arranging for cars and trailers to haul gear to meet us at the airport. Svein also arranged for a film crew to come along to document our adventure. Helping Svein was Kristin Moe Krohn another Norwegian. Kristin later joined us when we tried to climb Mt. Kilimanjaro in Africa. Her First Nation name was Angel Hands because she was really good at giving backrubs. Svein's name was Morning Bird because he always liked to rise early and make breakfast.

We flew out of Green Bay to Detroit, then to Amsterdam and then on to Oslo. The trip took about 12 hours and as is typical, we were tired when we landed in Oslo. Little sleep, too much food, and perhaps too much wine was not the best formula, but the excitement of being in Norway kept our energy levels up. For Corey and Chad, this was their second trip to Norway, and they relished that fact as they showed other first timers around the Oslo airport.

We quickly loaded our gear into cars, vans and trailers provided by Svein and headed north to the scenic and ancient city of Lom. It was T-shirt weather in Oslo and the fresh air felt great. We did have a scary event on our way to the mountain. After only about 30 minutes of driving, we came across a soldier with a rifle standing in the roadway pointing to tell us to turn off the highway and into a parking lot. It turned out that the Norwegian law was conducting a random search for drunken drivers. Each one of our drivers had to take a breathalyzer test. We were worried that there still might be some alcohol in the systems of the drivers but not to worry, they all passed with flying colors. We were duly impressed that Norway does not mess around with drunken drivers. If you are caught, you go directly to jail. It's not like Wisconsin, where it is not uncommon to hear about drivers being arrested 10 to 15 times before being incarcerated.

It took us the rest of this first day in Norway and the second to reach our base camp about 10 miles from Galdopiggen. There we met Sture and his climbing partners and prepared our rigs for the next day's start of the climb. Spring was coming to the Norwegian Mountain country with waterfalls popping out everywhere. The ice was just coming off lakes and rivers were flush with frothing water. More than once we drove right through waterfalls bouncing off the roadways.

The plan called for the wives and friends to start behind us on a different route a day after we would depart. Our plan was for all of us to summit at the same time, but the trekkers did not need to go at our very slow speed. In hindsight, we should have taken the same route, but Svein was in charge and the way he picked ended up working out OK. On the drive up to the starting point, we flushed a flock of ptarmigan, a mostly white grouse type bird that seems to thrive in a mountain or arctic environment.

Our actual start point was at the base of a ski hill. Even though it was mid-summer, the Norwegian National ski team was practicing on this hill. Our first 1,000 yards of climbing was directly up the ski hill. First, I would lead a pitch of rope, and then Sture would. We leap frogged up the mountain in good syncopation. This time, for lunch, we had good local cheese and sausage sandwiches along with energy drinks and bars.

Because we were in the north center of Norway, daylight was with us for about 16 hours a day and darkness was actually twilight. We got to see ancient volcanoes as we made our ascent. They were quite impressive with partially caved-in cauldrons.

After about 8 hours of climbing we made our night's camp in view of the summit, perhaps about 4 miles away. As we cooked dinner, the wind picked up and it started to snow. One goof up I made was to bring one less sleeping pad along and Corey ended up having to sleep without a cushion on the tent floor. I felt bad about that, but he dealt with it without whining one bit.

We woke up to blizzard conditions with visibility really limited. After eating some breakfast, taking down the tents and getting ready to push off, we made the decision to stay put until the weather improved. Therefore, we put the tents back up and burrowed in to wait out the storm. No sooner than we got in the tents did the wind calm down, the sun come out, and the temperature rise. So, once again we broke camp and started on our way.

Off in the distance we could see our wives, the blind climbers and guides trekking their way across a broad glacier named Styggebreen. Because we lost a few hours waiting out the storm, that group got way ahead of us and summited on their own. We met them when they were coming back down from the top. My wife Jane was not too happy about the climb, especially the narrow ledge they had to cross at the top of a glacier with a gaping crevasse waiting to engulf anyone unlucky enough to take a tumble. I was proud of her and my daughter-in-law Sara for reaching the top. After a few snacks and hugs they continued downward while we kept going upward.

After we crossed and went up the glacier, we had a series of steep pitches to the top of a knife ridge that divided the glacier in two. Once we crossed the ridge, things got a little dicey, as there was the very narrow ledge that Jane described. We had to traverse that narrow ledge for about 200 yards. I recalled the Trans-Sierra ski avalanche where I asked one of the photographers to help me cross. This time, my climb team helped me and Sture make the crossing. I went first, when we reached the end of the ledge I needed to make a sharp turn upward on the way to the summit. The guys set one more pitch of rope for me to snake up. When I got to the end, I was to wait until they returned from helping Sture cross the ledge. Stupidly, I unsnapped my seat belts and pulled my legs to the side so I could easily look down the mountain. All of a sudden I got very wary that I was only hanging by one static rope. One slip and I would be on my way down the slope while my Summiter sat safely roped in! Quickly, I re-positioned in the proper position and strapped myself back in. Now the chance of falling was greatly reduced. That reminded me of another bit of climbing wisdom. "There are old climbers and bold climbers, but there are no old bold climbers!"

At about 200 feet from the summit, the climb team set two rope pitches side by side so Sture and I could summit at the same time. We did not want to say either of us was the first to summit Galdopiggen, we both wanted to summit at the same time and we did.

A neat thing happened at the top. Svein, unbeknownst to us lugged a huge bottle of champagne in his backpack. It was a nice gesture, but no one was in the mood to drink alcohol at the summit. We decided to save it for a later date. We stayed at the summit for about an hour enjoying the view as the sun was still out and we were on the highest peak in the Jotunheimen National Park that was full of peaks.

We started down slowly. The slope was too steep to do the "dog sled" in reverse technique so my team let me down slowly 200 feet at a time by using climbing gear that played out the rope slowly and surely. Once we got past the narrow ledge area and back on the Styggebreen glacier the team hooked up two climbing ropes and assorted bags of gear that they latched onto the back of my Summiter. I then dug out ski poles and skied down the glacier for about a mile gaining huge chunks of distance on the rest of the team. I stopped when I got to the end of the glacier and waited in the growing twilight for them to catch up. This time, we took the way back that the other trekkers had taken. We only had about another mile to reach the cars at the base of the ski hill. To make things easier, we removed the Summiter apparatus from our sit skis and skied the rest of the way to the finish.

It was probably 10:00 pm when we arrived back at the hotel, where the head chef had baked a huge cake that looked like the mountain. Some of it was made of ice cream, so we even had avalanches when the ice cream started to melt.

We spent another six days in Norway seeing the country by car, boat and train. It was a great adventure, except for one thing. As usual, I got a good dose of bad sunburn on my face and some sores on my lips. What was alarming was that I could only feel the left side of my face, the right side was numb!

Chapter 17 - Climbing Mt. Whitney - The Rainbow Expedition

"Putting People with Disabilities on Top of the World"

When we returned from Norway after climbing Galdopiggen, I made an appointment with our family doctor to find out about the numbness on the right side of my face. It had not gone away. If anything, the numbness had worsened. The doctor wasted no time in sending me to a specialist. After a brief visit, he made arrangements for a MRI scan of my head. I still vividly remember meeting with the specialist in his office to review the results of the MRI.

Dr. Kaufman was blunt and to the point, which was fine with me. He told me I had a tumor smack dab in the middle of my brain right above my spine. The tumor, about the size of a grape, was probably benign but would kill me if I did not have it removed. The tumor was called an "acoustic neuroma". Dr. Kaufman gave me a couple of hospitals to check out that had experience in dealing of this kind of tumor. He said they were very slow growing and I had some time to review my options as long as I did not take too long.

By the end of the week, Jane and I made appointments with specialists both in Madison and Milwaukee. In the end, the decision on which way to go was pretty easy. In Madison, at the University hospital, they recommended surgery to completely remove the tumor. They said I would lose hearing in my right ear due to the surgery but that I should have a full and complete recovery. At Milwaukee, the treatment was to use a device called a "Gamma Knife" to radiate the tumor and shrink it. This would save my hearing, but there was no promise that the tumor would not re-generate. We choose the surgery option in Madison and scheduled it for a few weeks later in October.

I remember being pretty stoic about the whole issue until the day before surgery. We were in Madison for a series of tests. In one test, they wanted to try and get me to vomit by keeping my head still, but asking me to follow a red dot on a screen that darted up and down and right and left at an increasing speed. I beat that machine and apparently was one of the few persons to do it. However, later, in the parking lot after we were done for the day, I finally lost it and broke down and cried in Jane's arms.

The next day was the big day. I remember lying on a gurney in an elevator heading for the surgical floor. I felt fine, the numbness was not painful. I kept asking myself, why me? It did not take long and I was under the grip of the anesthesia.

I was in surgery for 13 hours as the doctors successfully removed the entire tumor. They said it was like peeling sticky wet paper off and in between a bundle of electrical wires. It was very tedious and dangerous work, but they got it done. Recovery was difficult and it took a couple of weeks before I was able to return to work. Not only had I lost hearing in my right ear for good, I was horribly disfigured on the right side of my face. This was something the surgeons had not mentioned before surgery. The surgeons had to slice through many facial nerves to get to the tumor and those nerves had to re-grow at a painstakingly slow pace. I could not close my eye completely and had to have a chunk of gold implanted in the eyelid, so my eye could shut better. Jane reminds anyone who wants to know how valuable I am with that chunk of gold in my eyelid. The disfigurement stayed with me for a long time. To this day, I can't chew on the right side of my jaw and it takes a huge amount of effort to smile, which to me looks more like a leer. It is common for me to tell new people I meet about this disability, because when I am passive, it looks like I am frowning. It is a constant struggle to present a happy face.

I was released from the hospital about 10 days later when I got sick with a urinary tract infection. I told the doctors it was time to get out of that place and continue healing at home. The doctors agreed.

Every day after getting home, I would go for long slow pushes in my everyday chair to re-build strength. It was time to put my belief in the outdoors as strong medicine back to the test. It was time to think about climbing another mountain. I wanted to see what would happen if I spent a bunch of time outside flirting with Mother Nature and her daughter, Danger.

What follows is a diary of my Rainbow Expedition's adventure on 14,505-foot Mt. Whitney in California (The highest peak in the lower 48 States). The goal was to put me on top of the mountain, a feat never even attempted by a wheelchair user. I have tried to reduce my competitive tendencies, but here I go again, trying to be first! After somewhat recovering from brain tumor surgery, it was time to get back to the mountains and see if I could still do the things I loved to do.

By the way, as far as I know, Whitney, again named for some surveyor, has no First Nation name like Tahoma. Because this mountain is nestled in a bunch of peaks, it took lots of measurements and study to determine that it was indeed the tallest in the lower 48 states.

We again used simple mountain climbing technology, (ropes, and ascenders, cross country skis, guides and rope setters) to climb the mountain by pulling myself up the rope in a specially adapted sit ski called the Summiter. Guides choose the straightest route up the mountain, irrespective of steepness but always cognitive of safety. Rope setters set 200 feet of static rope. called a pitch, anchored by at least three snow pickets (Long aluminum bars inserted in the snow, which act as anchors for the rope). As I climb, they set rope, while two other climbers set the next 200 feet of rope. The rope setters leap frog up the mountain always staying one rope pitch ahead of me.

People ask how many times I pull on the Summiter to climb. Well, I never have counted the number of times I have pulled on a length of rope, because my mind wanders and I get distracted from counting. But, if I pull one foot each time, that is 200 times for a length of rope, and there are about 26 rope sets in a mile of going up. So that represents about 5,200 pulls a mile and a 5-mile climb up will amount to about 26 thousand pulls total. Not too bad. As I said, I never counted until now when I am writing this chapter more than 14 years later.

Besides myself, the Whitney team included lead guide, Kurt Wedberg, (Sierra Mountaineering International) of Bishop, CA; Bill Ossofsky of Bishop, Senior Guide, and Zak Little of San Diego, Guide. Kurt and Zak were also my guides on the earlier Mt. Rainier climb in 1998. Helping out with support and gear hauling were my Son - Chad, Jim Wallen, and Dave Stubenvol who you remember also designed the Summiter and kept it in working order on the climb.

The Summiter frame was graced by a comfortable seat developed by the KI Corporation in Green Bay who also did a powder coated paint job on the apparatus. Not one, but two pairs of Peltonen Back County Skis were securely attached to the bottom side. The skis were to see a lifetime of use during the next 5 days, not only sliding over snow, but rocks and ice as well. In general, all our gear from Outdoor Industry sponsors worked great.

The months leading up to March 16th, 2001: The Wisconsin Team worked hard to get in physical shape for the climb by training to do relatively small amounts of work for long periods of time. This meant long swims, bike rides, runs and skis in the woods to build aerobic capacity. We all spent several hours a week in the gym weight training as well. Climb sponsors were also wooed for cash and product support. Meanwhile, in the Lone Pine/Bishop Area, lead guide, Kurt Wedberg spent time scouting and re-scouting the best route to the summit and also obtained the needed government permits and approvals to make the climb.

Friday, March 16th: The Wisconsin Team flew out of Green Bay to Los Angeles in the early evening and arrived in LA around 1:00 am. We rented a van and headed to Lone Pine, about four hours to the east. Sleep overtook us about 3:00 am, so we pulled over on the road and slept in the van untill daybreak at about 6:30 am.

Saturday, March 17th: We arrived in Lone Pine around 8:00 am and could easily pick out Mt. Whitney in the towering range just west of town. We drove up the Portal Road until we hit snow to do some scouting and gawking. We headed back to town, got some breakfast, a motel room and started the repeated tasks of packing and re-packing gear. We did take time out to do a TV station interview with local media at the request of local U.S.

Forest Service officials. This time we were on much better terms than on Tahoma.

The Wisconsin Team's JanSport internal frame backpacks are weighing in around 60 pounds. Heavy but manageable is what Chad states. I want to carry most of my own gear this trip, and my smaller JanSport "Bridger" daypack, which will hang on the back of the Summiter weighs in about 25 pounds. Equipment hanging on the outside of the packs is safely secured in Granite Gear Stuff Sacks. In addition, each climber carries two full 32 oz. Nalgene bottles, one filled with plain water and the other spiced with energy powder. Later in the climb, guide Zak Little shared his secret stash of Kool-Aid powder, that when mixed with melted snow, made an excellent energy drink in its own right.

Kurt, Zak and Bill show up about 10:30 p.m. with group gear (Food, stoves, full fuel bottles and cooking pots) which is parceled out to everyone. The Wisconsin packs now are weighing in at over 80 pounds. The team leaves Lone Pine at midnight and drives up Portal Road. At the snow line, gear is transferred into one 4-wheel drive truck. The plan is to try and drive through about one mile of snow covered road to reach a one mile length of south facing bare pavement, which would allow us to start the trek a bit closer to the mountain. The snow was too deep and no more vehicle progress could be made about ¾ of a mile from the uphill bare pavement.

I used my cross-country sit ski to ski up the road to bare pavement and then transferred to my wheelchair to push another mile on pavement to once again snow. I then left the chair behind and again skied up the rest of the road to the end at Portal Park.

All of this progress was up quite steep grades, but at this point is where the real climb began as did the very steep slopes leading to Mt. Whitney. The rest of the team ferried the Summiter and packs up the road to Portal Park. Snow on the road was soft and it was common to sink in over the knees. It did not take long to break out the Tubbs snow-shoes. For me, the road trip was difficult as the sit ski was very unstable in the soft snow. Tip overs were common place. By daylight, I was already sweaty and weary.

Sunday, March 18th: As dawn broke Sunday morning, the team began to ready the static climb ropes, furnished by Sterling Rope, for the day's journey through the pine forests. The terrain was steep and slopes tipped everywhere due to the large sun induced tree wells around each forest giant. The snow was deep and soon softened under the bright sunshine and above freezing temperatures. The warm Schoeffel Jackets and Saranac Hats and gloves were soon discarded in favor of light Polarmax t-shirts and lots of Dermatone sunscreen. The lofty goal for the day was to reach Lower Boy Scout Lake, but it was not to be. By 6:30 p.m., the team had just reached the canyon leading to Lower Boy Scout and hurriedly set up camp for the night, finishing just as darkness descended. The team had been climbing since 1:00 am in the darkness and bright sun, so after 18 hours of hard work and more than 40 hours without a good nights sleep, dinner was consumed quickly and sleep came easy and fast. Team members were snug and warm in Sierra Designs Expedition tents and sleeping bags. I was particularly comfortable using a Cascade Design inflatable travel pillow which held my head just right while sleeping and also had a liberal supply of Grabber Handwarmer's that added needed heat to my lower extremities, which cooled significantly during the later parts of the day.

The little hand warmers are a great invention of charcoal and iron filings that heat up when exposed to air. They produce heat for about six to seven hours. I would put some on my back and my neck at places that could warm my blood. I probably went through 50 of those little life savers during the climb and still use them to this day when I am outside in cold weather conditions.

Monday, March 19th: Kurt, knowing full well another long day was in store, rousted the team at 4:30 am in the cold chill of the predawn. Hot oatmeal and chocolate fueled the team and everyone managed to break camp and start upward just as daylight made its appearance. The going was relatively easy in the canyon while the snow remained firm and the first 10 rope pitches went quickly.

The Wisconsin Team began to learn the art of balancing and adjusting the heavy packs frequently to save energy and avoid serious injury by overuse of certain muscles.

However, the canyon was long and steep and it took until almost noon to break out on top at Lower Boy Scout Lake. A small part of the lake was open and brook trout were dappling the surface prompting Chad to wish he brought his fishing gear. Pan fried trout sure sounded good about that time. As we crested to Lower Boy Scout we were treated to an awesome sight of Mt. Whitney. Kurt pointed out our planned route and it looked scary and steep.

On the Summiter - Below Lower Boy Scout Lake

The rest break and easy going across the plain of Lower Boy Scout Lake were enjoyed for only a brief period of time as the steep slopes once again became an issue. We worked hard to get to our next camp site at Upper Boy Scout l Lake but again came up short and camped somewhere below Upper Boy Scout, but not far and everyone was pleased with the progress. Once again, camp was set up in the growing darkness and food and sleep came quickly.

Tuesday, March 20th: Again, up before daybreak, eat and break camp. The guys are getting good at this and it takes much less time for these chores. The trek begins even before daylight is in place. This was a long day of many steep pitches punctuated by traverses and some down hills as we position ourselves to get in place for the next day summit attempt. Jim and Chad at one point found themselves stuck on a narrow ledge, but a rope toss from Kurt got them back on safer footing after some nervous moments.

Everyone was fatigued, but there were still no major health or injury issues, a certain sign that our pre-climb training regime was on the mark. It seemed to me that the Outdoors truly was strong medicine!

We ended our day about 6:00 p.m. with three punishing steep pitches that put us at Iceberg Lake, again just beating darkness to set up our last camp site, get some food and hit the sleeping bags. Sleep time is short, as Kurt figures if we are going to make the summit and get back down in the daylight we will need to leave this camp by midnight. So, at 11:00 p.m., the dreaded wakeup call sounds through camp.

One gratifying aspect of this day is that the team can leave the camp in place and only need to carry a minimal amount of gear for the day instead of the very heavy full loads. Some extra clothes, energy food, water and crampons and our Princeton Head Lamps are all that is taken. The headlights show the way up the long and steep headwall leading to the summit. In the darkness, we all remember the interim goal today is to reach the notch at the top of this chute. The night before, Zak and I guess that it will take 8 pitches of rope to gain the notch.

Wednesday, March 21st: The team is ready to go at midnight. Guide Zak ropes up Chad, Dave and Jim and sets out on a steady pace. Snowshoes are left in camp and replaced with Grivel Crampons furnished by Climb High to gain better purchase in the steep snowfield. Kurt and Bill set the ropes for me.

Well, the eight pitch guess is not too far off. It actually took 10 rope pitches to gain the notch (a narrow, rocky gap that is barren of snow for about 20 feet). I left the Summiter for a spot on Chad's strong back. We both are roped in to the other climbers and everyone works darn hard to gain the needed 20 feet of distance through the notch and back on to snow. At 14,000 feet, the effort leaves everyone panting and resting. We are taking a break!

At this point, Kurt lets the team know that he has a good feeling about our chances of reaching the summit, but he says, he never promises anyone summit success until they actually make the top. How could anything be any harder than what we just went through and up? Looking down, no one can believe we actually climbed such steep pitches. I muse that I have never had to put so much faith and trust in Dave's design work and Kurt's guiding knowledge.

As we turned the short corner of the notch, we realize why Kurt said what he said. There are only three pitches to go, but its almost going to be straight up and for added measure, there is bare rock exposed in most sections because snow won't stick to such steep rock slopes.

It takes all of Bill's guiding skills to clamber up the slope and set the first rope. Zak then forges ahead and set the second and Kurt sets the third and final pitch that ends over a towering snow cornice at the summit. Well, for now, at least one of us is on top.

I am the first on the rope and start out, ever fearful of turning around and looking down. Fear and adrenaline power me up the last three pitches. However, this mountain does not give up its summit easily. The last 10 feet involved cresting a snow cornice (the flat top of the summit preceded by an almost straight up and down slope). The climb rope is dug into the snow and the front ski following the rope is also imbedded, preventing any forward progress. Kurt frantically digs away at the cornice sending chunks of ice and snow down on the rest of the climbers. Zak starts up from the second rope pitch to also help out. My wrists became soaked with liquid from blisters breaking on my fingers and palms.

Finally Kurt was able to break the rope and front of the skis free, and I, with strength just about gone, pulled myself over the cornice and on top of Mt. Whitney at about 11:30 am, almost 12 hours after leaving base camp and a total of four days after leaving the base of the mountain. The first time ever a wheelchair user has been at the top of this very high place.

Other members came up the ropes and collapsed with exhaustion after clambering over the cornice.

By noon, all were on top for the traditional handshakes, photos and sign in at the Summit Register. It was a beautiful day on top with a few scattered clouds, light winds and a temperature of about 35 degrees F.

Now the next phase of the adventure started; the descent. All the climbers descended the first three pitches backwards on the set ropes using the rappelling technique. I went down forward trying to balance as the guides paid out rope. The soft snow made this a tricky maneuver, and tipping over was not out of the question. In other climbs, the guides were able to construct a "dog sled in reverse" and merely walk me down the mountain. But in this case, the slopes were too steep and required a rope set every 200 feet all the way to base camp.

It took from 1:00 p.m. until 6:30 p.m. to reach base camp at Iceberg Lake. It was certainly a long but successful day; we had been at it for over 19 hours.

Thursday, March 22nd: Kurt was kind enough to let the team sleep in until 5:30 am! Wow, what a guy! By 7:00 am, the team was fed and packed and ready to continue down the mountain. Again, progress was fast while the snow was firm but the pace slowed considerably after the snow warmed under the hot sun. By noon, the team reached Lower Boy Scout Lake and stopped for a lunch break. We were still optimistic of reaching the cars by dark. But, due to very soft snow on the canyon and the needed extreme caution to make sure we did not break through the snow bridges covering the increasing melting streams of water in the canyon, progress dropped to a snail's pace. It took almost 4 hours to descend about 1,000 feet. At one point, Chad dropped a leg through the soft snow, pinning his ankle in unseen rocks below. The fall caused his heavy pack to push his face into the snow. Fast action by Dave and Jim to drop their packs and rush to Chad, pulling off his pack avoided suffocation. Everyone experienced similar "close calls" both up and down the mountain.

As darkness closed in, we had just gained the major tree line, still about one mile from the Portal Park and 4 miles from the cars. Serious examination of the alternative of setting a night camp was debated. The decision was made to press on in the darkness to make it out rather than expend our resources, setting up another camp in our growing state of exhaustion. The Wisconsin guys rose to the occasion by hustling out to the Portal, dropping packs and hiking back up the mountain to ferry out Kurt and Bill's heavy packs so they could more concentrate on setting ropes for me , now sitting on the Summiter for over 12 hours.

With everybody working together, we finally reached the Portal about 8:00p.m. We still had about 4 miles of road to hike out, but the fear and danger of falling or getting seriously hurt were gone. It was very hard work to walk down the road in soft snow, but at least we were still going down. All of the team was nearing total exhaustion except guide Bill Ossofsky, who carried his pack at a rapid pace to the cars, drove his truck back up the mountain as far as he could go and then set off to help the rest of us down to his truck. By 1:00 a.m., we had all reached bare ground and the vehicles to take us back to Lone Pine, a motel and outdoor hot tub. Boy did that feel good after spending over 22 hours descending from the Summit.

Friday, March 23rd: The day was spent sorting gear and drying out the wet stuff. It took four very long days to go up and over 22 hours to descend, yet sleep did not come easily until later Friday afternoon. The entire team realized that this was not just a hike up a hill, it was easily the most exhausting and dangerous thing any of us from Wisconsin had ever experienced. We were in awe of the Mountain and our respect for the mountain and our professional guides grew a great deal. The Mountain finally allowed us to the top, but not without tossing out obstacles every foot of the way. We escaped without serious or long lasting injuries and a rejuvenated bond connected all of us.

Rainbow Guides - Zak, Kurt & Bill

Climb Team member, Dave Stubenvol said it best in an email to me; "Brings back some fond memories and some not so fun ones as well. I know the physical challenge was the hardest that I've ever endured. Rainier and Norway were a piece of cake in comparison. That mountain fought us every inch of the way, as the decent was equally difficult as the climb. I remember well the terror I felt when we climbed out of the relative safety of the notch on to the last semi vertical face. I also recall digging fox holes to hide in when Curt started breaking an opening in the cornice. That ice went past us at 100 mph plus! A climb such as this one can only be understood and appreciated in the past tense. The complete exhaustion and lack of oxygen made the actual time spent on the mountain surreal, almost an out of body experience. Overcoming challenges and obstacles define us as human beings. Teamwork defines our character. To have shared this experience with friends is what I cherish the most."

We hope now to begin to enjoy the last part of this adventure and that is the memories of the trip and the inevitable question, of WHAT'S NEXT???

Chapter 18 - The Tallest Free Standing Mountain in the World - Going Up

Mt. Kilimanjaro in the east central African country of Tanzania at 19,340 feet is the tallest freestanding mountain in the world. From bottom to top, the trek would exceed 35 miles. Moreover, new climbing equipment for a wheelchair user would be in order. All of my previous climbs had been on snow, and Kili has no snow, except for a tiny glacier at the top of the top. Therefore, in September of 2003, we jumped on a plane, flew to Africa, and boldly attempted to climb this mountain.

In hindsight, I relied too much on second-hand information. We budgeted too little time and needed gear to make it to the summit. Had I known now what was needed, I think I could have made it to the top. Nevertheless, it was quite a trip and I was glad that I tried.

Our climbing team, the Rainbow Expedition, seemed to grow with each succeeding adventure. One of my son's began describing these trips as our "annual adventure of a lifetime!" This time, in addition to Corey and Chad, we had another close family friend, Tom Wilson. Also along again was our Storyteller, Connie Fellman and Angel Hands, our friend Kristen Moe-Krohn from Norway.

In addition, new to the team was my back surgeon, Bryan Pereira and his wife, Madeline. It was great to have two medical people along on this trip and it turned out I needed them more than I could imagine. Madeline was an anesthesiologist, so her First Nation name was "Dream Giver". Dr. Bryan was Medicine Man, but on the mountain he told people he was a shoe salesman, otherwise he would be pestered all of the time to treat the many ailments of the natives or in-experienced climbers. However, when he saw a true medical need, he did step up and help. He was a big help to us during and after the climb treating everything from blisters to administering altitude sickness medications to giving IV hydrating solutions.

Tom Wilson or "Chinook" our "quartermaster" did an excellent job of packing the team gear and more importantly, setting up a system so we know what was in each bag of luggage. We will be bringing much more gear than we will return with because of our successful efforts at finding clothing for our porters, guides and cooks. Tom says, "Jeff was convinced that we would not have enough room for all the things we were to take, but we ended up with an extra bag or two with nothing to put in them. (Polarmax, JanSport and Granite Gear all provided product for this project that we could share with our African partners.)"

We asked our many outdoor industry sponsors to provide clothing that we could leave behind and they did not disappoint us. After we returned from climbing, we distributed boxes of shirts and pants but sadly, the gear started showing up in the local market place a few days later. Money was more important to the porters than a clean shirt.

Actually, money was more important to us too. In planning for the trip, we thought we did not need much in the way of specialized gear to climb but we did need money for climbing fees, airline tickets, immunizations and things like that. To finance our climb we again sold T-shirts that were donated to us by JanSport. They did an excellent job on the design with a character of the mountain and the notation, "Rainbow Expedition – Putting People with Disabilities on Top of the World" across the top. While we sold a ton of shirts, we all had to dig deeper into our pockets to pay for this adventure.

Since there was no snow, I had to find another way to climb. We were told that the way we planned to take, called the Coca Cola route was easy and if we could handle the high altitude we should have no problem getting to the summit. While it might have been true we did not need ropes, ascenders or any other typical climbing gear we used in past climbs, I did need something like a wheelchair or bike I could use.

About this time, a company called One-Off came up a unique three-wheeled hand cycle with about 30 gears that was designed to climb. "One-Off is British slang meaning first of a kind. The odd bike, which I dubbed the Mountain Beast, had two wheels in the front and one in the back, which was the drive wheel. I kneeled on the Beast and rested my chest on a pommel and pushed and pulled on the pedals that where down in front of me. It had disk brakes and knobby tires. I did not like two main things about the Beast. It was very uncomfortable to be in for long periods and I mostly had to keep my head down looking at the ground because looking up for extended periods also hurt my neck. The only good thing about the Beast is that it could take me deeper into the woods and farther up hills than anything else then on the market.

I took delivery of the Beast about two years before we left for Kili. I broke a few things on it during training runs and it often slipped the chain when I was going uphill. I did not know until way after Kilimanjaro that the chain was mounted backwards. Remember, "I don't build them, I just drive them."

I took the Beast to Mt. Bross in Colorado for an unsuccessful second attempt at summiting that mountain. We had to turn back because of blizzard conditions near the top. I tell about that trip in Chapter 20. Moreover, instead of using my regular handcycle, I rode the Beast all over the neighborhood and on the sledding hills at a Green Bay Park called Bairds Creek. This park had the tallest hills within twenty miles of home and was the place we worked out with the Summiter in winter. As much as I tried to condition myself to tolerate resting on the pommel, I never really did enjoy riding the Beast.

To ride the Beast in Tanzania I had to get special permission from their government as climbing is typically limited to walking. I had to use the USA embassy to wade through the bureaucracy but we finally did get permission.

By September 22 the work was about done. All the planning, fund raising, work outs, equipment preparation, team building, organizing, visa getting, special permissions from the Tanzanian government, (to allow me to use wheels on the mountain) had been completed. We even received approval from Northwest Airlines, to allow me to fly with an oversized package that held the disassembled Beast.

Connie says, "It's finally here! I can hardly believe this day has come. The countless hours of training and preparation are going to pay off! Training to climb a mountain can be a lonely endeavor, in my view. Ask your friends now if they would spend a Saturday climbing up and down ski hills for hours and see how many takers you have. Yeah, me too! But I found it gave me great time for reflection alone. I felt muscles in my body I never knew I had and saw things in nature I never would have otherwise. The simple beauty of a doe munching on a bright red maple leaf...spectacular. Isn't this what it's all about?"

Today, September 23, we leave for Africa. We fly from Green Bay to Detroit then to Amsterdam and then all the way to Mt. Kilimanjaro International Airport in Tanzania. It will be about a 20-hour trip from take off to landing. Everyone is meeting at my house to load up and head to the airport. Well, everyone but Connie. She is flying in from Lansing and will be waiting for us at the airport.

Our house is a busy place with last minute packing, TV and newspaper interviews and wondering what we might have forgot.

Connie says, "I have taken a job in Lansing Michigan and I had to fly back to Green Bay to join the team. I cannot express the joy it is to see my climb team again. What a great feeling to see these orange climb team shirts stream into the airport in Green Bay. I am home! The splendid group dynamics of this team are apparent from the start. Each with our own strengths blending together very well in an instant warmth of friendship."

Leaving the USA was a bit nerve wracking. Previously I had obtained the dimensions of the airplane's cargo doors from Northwestern Airlines. I took the Beast to a package store and ordered up a cardboard box big enough to fit the taken apart Beast, but small enough to fit into the plane cargo door.

After we checked in and were doing interviews with local media, an airlines agent found me and told me the box the Beast was in would not fit by three inches. They brought the box back down to us and we set to work to somehow make the box less tall by a bit more than three inches. This was in the era of high airport security. Do you think we could find a knife or scissors anywhere? The agent finally found a scissors, a knife and wrapping tape. We quickly cut the box open. When we did that, a bunch of those plastic peanut insulation cubes spilled all over the floor. What a mess! To keep this saga from getting any longer, suffice to say we lowered the height of the box, re-taped it, and sent it back to the airplane. This time, it fit. However, it was not the last time those plastic peanuts were to see the light of day. Northwest Airlines is no more, but many thanks to their employees who helped us with the box and the corporation who donated the cost of shipping the Beast to and from Africa.

We did experience our second crisis in Detroit, when Connie forgot her ticket envelope on the plane we flew in from Green Bay. By the time she realized the tickets were on the plane, the plane had left Detroit. After a frantic time of running from place to place in the airport and plunking down another $100, she got replacement tickets, which I think she clutched in her hands the rest of the trip. Tom says, "I am beginning to wonder if Connie is like my brother Jay, an absent minded professor."

Connie says, "After two speedy scampers through airports in stocking feet (hiking boots not highly recommended for airport security)... one to retrieve my video camera that drove away from the Lansing airport, another to get new tickets in Detroit to continue on to Africa... I am considering changing my Indian name to "Swift Socks."

The flights to Africa are fine, on our stop in Amsterdam we picked up Kristin who flew in from Norway a few hours earlier. Hugs all around and I can tell, we have assembled a great team.

I am worried about Corey; he has a cold and a terrible cough. Poor guy, what a time for this to happen. Speaking of colds, I have not had one in about 3 years, and it seems like for the past few days, I am getting one too.

September 24th is my birthday, now in Amsterdam, I turned 55. I guess we might have a beer in Africa to recognize that I made it to 55!

The flight from Amsterdam to Tanzania is neat in that the plane is quite empty and we all spread out in empty seats to take naps and catch up on lost sleep.

Connie says, "Awakened from sleep on flight to the call; "Is there a medical doctor on board? A medical doctor please to aisle 51!" I feel a surge of pride as I see two Rainbow Expedition T-shirts fly down the aisle. Bryan and Madeline jump to the rescue. They've begun saving lives before we ever even reach Africa! I'm tremendously proud and grateful to be a part of this team. "

When we land in Tanzania, (Mt. Kilimanjaro Airport) it is dark, windy and humid. I would guess the temperature is in the high 60's. Connie says,

"We've been flying for nearly 20 hours, but finally we are approaching Kilimanjaro... the city, not the mountain. I didn't even realize there was a city by the same name! Here's starts a glorious journey of discovery. The first thing we notice is the lack of lights surrounding the airport. I think I spotted eight total. We're not flying into a metropolis here. This is when it really sinks in for me. I'm in Africa!"

We pretty much shoot through customs in a short time and finally meet our hosts. I can tell, Bryan has been to these types of places before, not sure what he did for the customs agent, but boy, did we go through that place fast. Connie says, "Preceding through customs it becomes apparent the African official does not care for the Beast box. It's a mystery unspoken amongst the team, but somehow or other Bryan was able to get the Beast through customs. The journey of discovery takes a short break, some things are better not known. It's here, that's what counts and we are grateful."

Moses, who has become a great friend, is the leader of the group who is there to take us to the Capricorn Hotel where we will stay when not on the Mountain. We pack the Beast in its box on top of a van and try to tie it down securely. We had to reopen the box here at Customs, something that will haunt us in a short time.

Tom, Connie and I jump in a Land Rover with Moses and follow the rest of the team out of the parking lot for about an hour of driving to the Capricorn. At one point, I see what appear to be large white butterflies flittering across the dark highway. Moses is puzzled, as he has never seen them before. All of sudden there are clouds of them…what is going on? Then we realize…the Beast box is tearing open in the wind and the "butterflies" are actually the foam peanuts used as insulation for shipping. What a way to announce our entrance into Tanzania by littering 60 miles of highway with white foam peanuts! Connie says, "You wouldn't think it, huh? But here we were driving through amazing scenery even in the dark of night. Small shacks dot the roadway, some with the benefit of electricity, some not. Occasionally we see a cluster of locals gathered on a front porch telling stories. It's like another time altogether and it's amazing. While gasping at the spectacular starlit night out the window, we suddenly find ourselves in the midst of an African blizzard! Wait... that's not snow? Those are foam peanuts flying out of the Beast box falling apart on the vehicle in front of us! Stop!" There is nothing we can do and Moses says, not to worry about it.

The ride in the dark is still nonetheless interesting. They drive on the "wrong" side of the road and there are no stop signs or stop lights. Just speed bumps and round a-bouts. We pass small villages with what appear to be brick houses. Once in awhile we see electric fluorescent lights over the buildings and many people are still up hanging out in small groups on porches. It is late, like about 11:00 p.m.

When we arrive at the Capricorn, a guard opens the gate and we drive in the parking lot. We are greeted at the front desk with a papaya drink and welcomes from the hotel staff. Our rooms are around the back, down a narrow trail. We are two to a room and find them quite comfortable with running water, electricity, real toilets and tubs with showers. We each have a veranda looking out over jungle type vegetation. Corey is my roomie and he jumps in the shower while I do some unpacking.

Connie says,"Unbelievable luxury in this impoverished area of the world; we've arrived at Capricorn Hotel. Lush rain forest with streams and water-falls trickling through the grounds, and to cap it off flushing toilets and hot showers. Wow, what a welcome. Oh, by the way... has anybody seen my bag?" Tom says, "Connie's "big bag" is not with us and I am the "Quarter Master" and responsible to see that everything is with us. Fortunately, her bag shows up the following morning – much to my relief!"

The team convenes shortly and we hike back to the main hotel and quickly learn the bar is still open and we are introduced to a light and very tasty local beer aptly named Kili. Our team doctor gives us the OK to down some carbohydrates to celebrate our safe arrival and my birthday. Connie says, "We unwind over a Kilimanjaro beer before turning in for a much needed rest. Happy Birthday Rainbow. How fitting that you turn the speed limit in this glorious place with these phenomenal people." After two or three rounds, it's back down the trail and it does not take long for us to drop off to sleep.

Connie says, "Jolted awake from a sound doze by what sounds like a screaming baby.... or is it a bird?.... or a monkey??? Whatever it is it sounds like it's right on our porch! The cattle, lambs and roosters wake us more gently in the morning. I can't imagine a place more beautiful."

Our plans for today are to unpack and pack and take a tour of the local Village, Marango. After Breakfast, we meet Alfred another person who quickly becomes our friend. It turns out Alfred will be climbing with us. Once, many years earlier, Alfred climbed and summited Kili, so it will be good to have him along with us.

As we leave the Capricorn on foot, we begin to see many natives heading down the road to market. Many of them are carrying heavy loads on their heads, from bunches of bananas to 5-gallon plastic pails of stuff. Just across from the hotel is a "meat market". This consists of a shed, with a side of beef hanging in the shade. If you want some, the shopkeeper waves off the flies, chops off a chunk and hands it to you. No refrigeration, no nothing! Most Tanzanians in this part of the country are from the Chugga Tribe. The Massi tribe is concentrated in other parts of the Country although we think we spot a few of them due to their unique red and blue robes and tall stature. Most walkers carry sticks. When asked why, the answer was for snake protection!

The local kids are very friendly and are fond of coming up asking for a pen. It seems early missionaries to this part of the world gave pens and pencils away and little else, so these kids have learned to beg like those before them.

Every women or girl we see is wearing a traditional "dress". Men wore a variety of clothes from suits to shorts, tank tops and sandals. As dusty as this place seems to be, how they keep their clothes so clean is a mystery.

We hiked out of town up to waterfalls with an interesting traditional story. Seems there was a young girl who became pregnant before getting married. Since this was taboo, she was about to be executed, but was spared her life by a benevolent judge. Shortly afterward, she was at the waterfalls getting water when a lion approached her. She kept backing up and went right over the falls to her death. The morale to the story was if you break the rules, you would pay no matter what! Right in the middle of the top of the waterfalls is a statue of the maiden and back in the bush is a statue of the lion. Pretty neat! Tom says, "We have a young African lad, about 8 or so, that climbs up a ways on the water falls and plunges into the water. He does this several times and we are about to give him some money but are told by Alfred told not to because he is a "drug addict" and will only make his situation worse."

We stopped at the Village Market to shop. Kristin bought a couple of the wrap around dresses. One was for my wife Jane. Kids chewed on sugar cane and the adults wandered from shop to shop. Sometimes, there was not really a shop, just a pile of shoes or clothes on the ground. One woman was selling bras from a large pile on the ground. Potential buyers would try them on over their other clothes right in front of everyone. . We also learned the word "Jambo" It meant a whole bunch of things, but mainly you used the word when you met someone or thanked them for something. Another unusual thing was the way they told time. The daily clock started at sunrise, which was twelve o'clock.

Connie says, "Adorable children run to the roadway as we pass with a big smile and friendly "Jambo". Their faces pull on a heartstring you never knew you had. A little girl in a party dress and just one flip-flop skips along with us most of the way and I can see a little boy's toes poking out through the sneakers he's far outgrown. Their warm, bashful eyes and dazzling smiles are one of my most vivid memories of Africa."

Connie continues, "Yet, as amazing as this scene is to us...we are the spectacle here. It seems that no one in this village has seen a wheelchair before. Unabashed stares follow us through the village as Jeff moves along. We learn that disabled people here generally stay in their homes, until they die. They can't afford wheelchairs.

The homes themselves are both fascinating and shocking, ranging from mud huts to modern structures left partially built. Most are surrounded by dirt not grass and we see women peeling vegetables and washing clothes in a stream. Nestled in the jungle just off the road smoke rises from other homes and you see a steer or goat tethered to a stake... though Alfred tells us some livestock still stay inside the home as it used to be. He takes us to one of the original huts built in the 1950's and still standing. Inside we see the livestock area and beds where the family slept. The entire thatched roof structure is about half the size of our hotel rooms!

I've just heard the comparison that what the average American pays for a cup of coffee at Starbucks could feed one of these villagers for a month! The comparison makes me feel like a fat, ugly American... but the warmth radiating from these beautiful people is genuine and sincere. Rarely have I felt such graciousness."

We then jumped in the back of a pick-up truck and drove about three miles to a blacksmith shop. Wow, talk about primitive. The workers were making spears for the Massi tribe. They used what appeared to be old inner tubes to fan the charcoal flames in which the metal was heated. They used bare hands to push the coals together, ouch. Some of our team bought some spear replicas to hang on the wall back in Wisconsin. The Blacksmith Shop Foreman had only one old sheet of newspaper to wrap our purchases in. So, he kept tearing off small pieces for wrapping. Tom says, "If this is the way these young men make a living, it is really something. The time and effort - and danger that surrounds them constantly - is what we used to think were the "old days" in the U.S."

The rest of the day was spent getting organized for tomorrow, when the actual climb begins. And, just great, my cold seems to be getting worse with a stuffed up nose and tickle in my throat. Our evening meals were quite grand. Our waiters were formally dressed and impeccably "proper" in an old English sort of way. The food was of a meat and potatoes variety and very tasty. Every meal had lots of bread, which was very good. Breakfasts were also traditional American, with bacon, eggs and toast the usual fare. Bryan made sure we only drank "purified" water or from bottles that had sealed caps. He had brought along a gallon sized purifier that he would dump sealed water bottles in to double purify our drinking water.

To climb Kilimanjaro, it was required by the Tanzanian government that you hire porters to carry your gear and cook your food. That was ok with us. We also had a local guide, Bryson, to deal with all of that and point us in the right direction, which was more or less up. African porters are not paid much, about $3.00 per day on the mountain. Moreover, at this small wage, a porter on Kili made more in a year than an elementary school teacher.

After Breakfast, we went for a short hike down the road to a point where we could see Mt. Kilimanjaro's summit in the distance. This is the first time we have actually been able to see the top.

We finish our packing and go through a process of saying good bye to the hotel staff, doing some local media interviews and then driving up the road about 2 miles to the Marangu Gate, which is the start of the climb. At the National Park headquarters, we fill out the necessary paperwork and meet our guides, porters and cooks, which all together, amounted to 25 additional people on our team. These guys haul all the cooking gear, food, our gear, my wheelchair, water, fuel and their own gear up and down the mountain. Normally, most of them hike a lot faster than the climbers. They get to the day's destination, pick out, reserve the best available shelters, and begin preparation for the evening meal.

Climb day started with more paperwork at the Park Entrance. To get to the tables of the processors there was one step that Chad helped me jump up. (This was not a place or time for me to whine about accessibility!) Chad and I had a freak accident that almost ended the adventure before it started. Just as I was about to get on the Beast, Chad helped me down a small set of steps. When I bounced down, I lost my balance and started to fall forward. Chad made a desperate attempt at catching me, but we both hit the pavement hard. As I fell, I pushed Chad's head into the pavement as I bounced off a curb and then dropped another five feet into a rock filled ditch. I cannot believe I was not hurt in anyway. Other guys on the team jumped in the ditch and hauled me out. This was right in front of officials and dignitaries who were there to see us leave. Yikes, what a poor start to display to all those onlookers. However, this was just a harbinger of things yet to come. Tom says, "This is not the way to start a trek up the mountain. We are doing this with a disabled person - and we can't even get to the trail before we have our first accident. Chad's head ached for most of the day – I think that he was actually knocked out for a while."

The big sign welcoming climbers had a warning message that was somewhat scary for Corey and me. It warned climbers not to climb to the top if you had a cold or fever. We had to ignore the message after flying half way around the world; this would be our only kick at this cat.

In our trip planning, we put lots of effort into making sure we knew what obstacles we had to overcome to reach the summit of Kili. All our data, led us to believe that altitude acclimatization would be one of the hardest things to deal with. We also where led to believe the trail would be an easy hike except for the constant going up. Boy, were we wrong.

About 100 feet from the start of the trail, we came across a ditch about 20 inches wide and 15 inches deep. The front end of the Beast dropped into the ditch and there it stayed. Some of the team quickly reached down and lifted me and the Beast out of the ditch and away we went again, but for only about another 100 feet when we faced a step that again the Beast could not get over. Once again a quick lift and away we went, only to face yet another insurmountable obstacle in less than 100 feet. All the lifting, pushing, and pulling caused the front chain on the Beast to come off track. Madeline and Chad went to work to free the chain and then re-track it back on the gears. The chain was really stuck and it took about 20 minutes to get things fixed. I peddled about 10 turns and the chain came off and jammed again. Wow, less than 100 yards from the start, and looks like we are in big trouble. Tom says, "We have gone about 200 yards and it has taken us about an hour. Our guides must be wondering what to hell we think we can do. I begin to wonder if this trip was going to be over before it got started – and I know that Jeff is frustrated and Madeline is really questioning the reliability of the bike."

Bryson, our lead guide suggested we jump up a steep hill to a service road that would get us half the way to our first campsite on a friendlier track. The road would not have the steps and ditches like the trail, so Corey jumped me on his back and scrambled up the hill to the road where the Beast was waiting. After several other fits and starts, we seemed to get in a moving rhythm and started to make some progress.

It was a nice sunny day with temperatures in the 70's and now we were moving. We did stop a few times for snacks and breaks and once to take pictures of monkeys in the trees above us. It's hard to say who was watching who with more interest, us or the monkeys?

When we reached the end of the road and picked up the trail, things got miserable once again. For a while, Chad or Corey carried me on their backs. Eventually we decided that I would use my wheelchair and a porter would carry the Beast to the Mandara Camp Site. It took Corey, Chad and Tom about four back breaking hours of lifting, pushing and pulling me in the chair up a most inhospitable trail full of ditches, steps, rocks and tree roots. At least the trail was dry and we did not have to deal with mud, but that was a small consolation. Tom says, "This trail was a "bitch" and I wondered how long Corey, Chad and I would be able to keep up the pace. My thoughts were wondering from "how do I do this for the rest of the day" to "this must make Jeff feel like he has no independence at all". Were there any insects you ask? Not really.

104

We did enjoy what was to be a delightful daily occurrence, and that was Afternoon Tea. Out of nowhere, one of the cooks produced a hot thermos of tea and great tasting cookies on a silver platter. Talk about luxury in the middle of the jungle, what a contrast.

Just before dark, we crawled into Mandara Camp. This place was a series of A-frame huts used mainly for sleeping. One big shelter was used for dining. We arrived in the waning daylight and realized we, at 9,500 feet, were above the clouds. Tom says," I was beginning to wonder if we would ever get to this spot. The shelters were actually better than what I envisioned."

We quickly dumped our gear in our assigned huts and hurried off to dinner. Dinners on the climb were always great with a wide variety of foods. We usually started with a snack like popcorn or hot peanuts and tea or coffee. The main course was usually some meat in gravy, vegetables, and rice or potatoes. Desert was usually fresh fruit. We often lingered over desert talking about the day's events and what might happen tomorrow.

Another nightly ritual was having Kristin and Corey set up the Satellite Phone. We planned ahead of time that Corey would have priority, if our calls were limited, to call his wife Sara who was pregnant with their second baby. Sara also had a pipeline set up to update our WEB site, and call other team member family to update them. (Sara and Corey had baby daughter Zoey Rane on November 22, 2003) As Kristin and Corey became more familiar with the Sat Phone, we all had quite a few opportunities to call back to the States and surprise our loved ones back home.

Chad, Corey, Tom and I shared one hut and Kristin, Connie, Madeline and Bryan shared the other. The huts were quite comfortable and we all slept well. The huts had battery lighting that dimmed after a time and no heat. But, with temperatures only dipping down into the 50's, sleep came easy. Tom says, "I knew that sleep would be difficult for me because I had overexerted myself during the days climb and past experience told me that my body would not settle down to sleep for a long time - so I took one of my sleeping pills about every 2 hours during the evening. I did get some sleep and was one of those (probably the one) who released more gases than one should be allowed. (Most of the time, I should say we slept well except for the occasional passing of gas, not only in the huts but on the trail by some of our team who will remain un-named. But let's just say, it was not only the guys who once in awhile stunk up the place!"

September 27th, Saturday - I woke up with a full fledged cold, runny nose and sore throat. Just great. Nevertheless, there is nothing I can do, but press on.

 When it was time to get up, all the team hiked to the dining hut for breakfast except me dealing with my cold that had become even worse. Moreover, Corey's coughing was not getting any better either.

You should know that the toilets in Africa were usually a simple hole in the ground over which one squatted to do the duty. You can imagine how difficult this would be for a wheelchair user. In a magnificent display of invention, before leaving Wisconsin, I took my wheelchair to Williams Canvas in Green Bay. Those artists in cloth cut a hole in the fabric of my seat base in the shape of a toilet seat and then covered it with a Velcro sealing fabric. All I had to do was remove my seat cushion, and viola, I had a toilet. Mornings in the hut became my time to do my duty, as I was not much of a breakfast eater anyway. This little invention will be used lots on other outdoor adventures I plan to take, as finding toilets in the outdoors is one tough problem. In fact, the women on this trip used my wheelchair when bathroom time called.

Today's trek was about 15 miles and was more of the same from yesterday with steps, ditches and rocks with a good measure of dust and dirt tossed in. I used the chair and a porter carried the Beast on his head up to the next camp, Horombu.

The terrain started to change into fewer trees and more Savannah. We saw lots of neat wild flowers and probably hundreds of other climbers coming down off the mountain.

I took another pounding in my chair. The guys did the best they could lifting me up over the obstacles but crashing down on the other side was routine. A couple of times I tipped over backwards and one time broke my sunglasses against Chad as we all went down in a heap in the dust. Tom had a spare pair of prescription glasses that ended up better than the ones I broke. I still use them…thanks Tom!

At one point, Alfred pointed out a high mountain coming into view that was not Kilimanjaro. It was called Mawenzi and was the second highest mountain in the Country and apparently very difficult to climb. In the 1950's, an airplane crashed into the side of the mountain and it is still there and quite visible. Apparently, it is in such a dangerous place, no one has ever climbed to it for any sort of retrieval.

Boy, did we look forward to afternoon tea! We did not want to get up and start moving again, but we wanted to make the next camp before dark. Tom says, "This was probably the hardest day from a physical exertion standpoint in my entire life. I have backpacked elk from the Flattops in Colorado, baled over 2000 bales of hay in a day, tossed sheep around all day, spent 14 hours roofing in the hot sun - but this effort to get Jeff to Horombo was the most physically demanding thing that I can remember – and I considered myself in good physical shape."

Horombu Camp, (12, 500 ft) was similar to Mandara, only starker as there were no trees to speak of. For a while, we were able to see down the Mountain to the plains below, but most of the time, we looked down on solid cloud cover.

A treat after another hard day was Kristin going over to the Porter Camp to purchase bottles of Coca-Cola. Dang, that tasted pretty good with dinner. Speaking of dinner, I think our team had the best cooks on the Mountain. We always had a fancy dining cloth, hot food and water for tea or coffee, a wide variety of dishes. We had one group next to us with just a big pot of noodles, while we had a plate of fish, one of chicken, veggies and lots of fresh bread and butter. Tom says,"My body hurt all over and the backrub from Kristin was phenomenal relief! I asked the "medicine man" for a "pill" to help me relax. I don't know if I slept that night but I definitely relaxed – again including my colon valve to the dismay of my shelter partners."

Tomorrow is going to be a rest and recovery day, so we stayed up a bit longer to talk and enjoy the moment. One common feature that we Americans don't do especially well, is hang out and just talk. The Africans are very good at that. I coined that as "porch sitting". All over the place, wherever there is habitation, it seems African's like to hang out, watch the world go by and talk about it to their companions. I am vowing to do more of that, both here and when I get home.

September 28th, Sunday as planned, this was to be a rest and recovery day. We slept in a bit later and then worked on gear. Chad took a hike up the trail we would be on tomorrow and reported that maybe I should jump back on the Beast instead of the wheelchair. We did some more adjusting on the Beast and I took it for a test run up the trail. It seemed to work better, with a tether in the front and next to each rear wheel. (The first day proved to me that this trip was not going to be one of those independent adventures, where I allowed no one to help me. If that had been the rule, I still would be on the first mile of the trip rather than 20 miles into the trip.)

The highlight of my day was my first attempt at "porch sitting". I sat on the edge of our hut with a full hydration unit of grape cool aid and watched the world go by. I had a steady stream of visitors including a little mountain chipmunk who really liked the roasted peanuts I fed him.

September 29th, Monday we hit the trail relatively early with our goal to reach Kibo Hut. Bryson said the first half of today's hike was much like yesterday, but after that, the trail smoothed out and the going would be easier.

We made it about 100 yards when the darn Beast broke down again. But, once again, Madeline and Chad fixed whatever was broken and on we went. Tom says, "This damn bike was not what it was cranked up to be and the pre-climb information about the condition of the trail was not even close to being accurate - or at least we had interpreted it much differently. However, this was intended to be a hell of a challenge and I am one who liked to challenge my physical ability. I began to believe that Kili was going to put me through one ----ing good test." All agreed, it was much easier to bounce the Beast up the rocks than the wheelchair like the past two climb days. And, I agreed. Now, instead of Corey in the rear lifting, he assumed the role of Lead Dog and pulled from the front. A pack frame hip belt supplied by JanSport really proved valuable in saving Corey's skin as it took much of the brunt of the snap of the haul rope when it went taunt.

True to Bryson's word, about half way, the trail became rock free and the going got better. We were climbing at a steady pace, too bad the whole trail was not like this part. Whenever a cloud enveloped us, the temps dropped and we added clothes, and when the cloud scurried past us, the sun would once again convince us to shed layers until the next cloud happened by.

We reached Kibo hut, (16,000 feet) late in the day, but had enough time for everyone to make some Sat Phone calls and make final preparations, for late tonight we leave for the summit, which we can see very easily. Our accommodations at Kibo consisted of one large room with bunk beds and dining table. Our plan was to rise about 1:00 am and actually start climbing about 2:00 am.

We talked with other climbers who were going no further because of altitude problems. We all felt pretty good. Kristin, who had not taken any meds up to this point, did pop one pill from Bryan to quell a headache. Alfred was also having headache problems.

We all were a bit nervous in anticipation. It had been over two years in the making to reach this spot and it was time to "go for broke". The trip was emotional in one respect in that sometimes it seemed quite hopeless that I would get very high, and then a good chunk of altitude was knocked off and my optimism soared. Tom says," I was trying to figure out how I could tell Jeff, Corey and Chad that if I personally was going to have any chance of making it to the summit of Kili – I was starting to get a headache too – that I would not be able to assist Jeff from Kibo to the summit. This was a personal dilemma for me. I wanted to be there for Jeff but knew that I would likely suffer physical exhaustion if I tried to provide the same support for Jeff at 15,600 plus feet that I had done from 6,000 to 15,600 feet. I finally got enough "balls" to just tell him that I couldn't continue to help lift, carry and drag him and the bike. That was tough for me, as I felt I might be very selfish leaving Corey and Chad, and the guides and porters to help my very close friend Jeff pursue the summit of Kili."

September 30th, Tuesday we woke at the appointed hour and got dressed, ate some breakfast and started to climb as planned at about 2:00 am. The stars were out with just a slight wind with temperatures probably around 25 degrees. Madeline, Connie, Bryan and Tom headed out in the lead with some guides. Corey, Chad, Bryson, Alfred, two other guides, and myself followed. In order to make sure the Beast did not slip its chain again, I stopped quite frequently to check and tighten if needed the hex nuts holding the second drive system in place. We quickly reached 17,000 feet. It was tough, but we made steady progress as the eastern sky started to lighten up. Ahead at about 17,400 feet was the Hans Meir Cave. (A small indentation in the side of the mountain that the first summited overnighted in back around 1870.) There was a metal sign affixed to the cave, and the rising sun made the sign a bright beacon we aimed for. The slope was steep, but worse than that was the soil on the trail. It was becoming like small marbles. The Beast's tires were sinking lower and lower in this scree and all my helpers were having a harder and harder time helping me move upward.

Tom says, "The stars above Kili were numerous and it looked like we could reach out and touch them. Numerous "shooters" were seen as we looked up once in a while rather than at the feet of person ahead of us on the trek upward.

The morning sun was fantastic as we viewed it come over the horizon and shine on the clouds and rocks below us. The cold would get my feet and hands if we stopped for too long a time because my circulation to the extremities of my body are not good in the cold – my platypus froze up and had to drink water from the Nalgene bottle. I could see Gilman's Point – and some of the headlights of climbers that had started earlier than us that same morning - and wondered if we ever would get there. We kept going back and forth across the scree. My headache was gone and physical exercise and cold crisp air was clearing my head and my colon both. I really felt sorry for the porter-guide behind me because the odors must have been unbearable."

We finally reached the cave and took a break. I jumped off the Beast and had a few Cliff Bars and Gels. As usual, we shared our energy foods with the guides who seemed to really like the stuff as much as we did. The last hundred feet of so was really hard and I was ready to throw in the towel. My team was really starting to suffer because of me. It was one thing to work so hard at lower altitudes, but it was another thing this high up. Corey was still coughing badly. But, Corey especially would have none of me quitting. He scouted around above the cave and insisted we keep going. So, we did. The mushy soil just got worse and worse until finally at 17,500 feet, the wheels on the Beast were buried to the hubs and it took supreme effort by everyone to get me to move even another inch. So, it was over for me. But that was ok. We all knew going in that the goal was to get as high as we could and that is what we did. We took some photos and with hugs all around. Corey, Chad, and one guide kept going up while the rest of us descended back to Kibo Hut to wait out the drama above us.

Tom says, "We got word via our talk-a-bouts that Jeff had make it as far as the "beast" and his helpers would allow him to go. He was buried to the axel in the scree and there was no way his sons, porters, and guides would be able to get him further. That was tough - again because I felt that I should have been there helping him instead of going on ahead with the other team members. My consolation was that Jeff told Corey and Chad to go on and try to reach us and the summit and he (Jeff) would go back to Kibo Hut to wait for us. We could see Corey gaining on us from below and we could see Chad struggling with his bad knees and ankles. I felt for him immensely.

The climb to Gilman's Point was never ending. We could see the rocks and people standing on this false summit and kept wondering if we would get there. Madeline has a terrible upset stomach and I thought that she would "blow lunch" any minute but she kept up the pursuit. We finally reached Gilman's Point – Corey way ahead of the rest of us – and I realized that there was no way in hell that we would have been able to help get Jeff to this location. The steep rocks would have required other type of equipment and I don't believe that even Corey, the strongest and most determined person I have ever met, would have been able to shoulder Jeff up these rocks. I thought about the persons who had been so influential in my life and now passed, my dad (Jim Wilson), my cousins Lloyd Johnson and Nate Wiese - and asked them to give me the strength to continue. These three men were my heroes and some of my best friends."

Connie says, "Climbing through the scree that stopped Jeff was terrible. It was one step forward and two back. It was like wading uphill through quicksand. We were already at an elevation that provided only 50% of the oxygen that is back at the start of the climb. No matter how fit you are, the altitude is brutal."

Tom continued, "When we finally reached Gillman's Point, the view was spectacular! The volcanic ash in contrast with the 150 to 200 foot glaciers and the blue ski was a site to behold. I finally believed that the summit was possible for at least some of us. I really didn't think that Madeline would make it and if she chooses not to go further, I knew that Bryan would stay with her. After the rest of the team headed up toward the summit, we again heard via our talk-a-bouts that Bryan and Madeline were also on their way up and Madeline was still not sick.

As we reached the summit, the view was again fantastic! The bright sun, the blue sky, the white-blue glaciers, the idea that we had reached the highest point on the continent of Africa brought goose bumps and a smile. I had accomplished something that in my wildest dreams I had never thought about ever attempting – let alone accomplish. I just wish that Jeff would have been there to share it with the other seven members of our Rainbow team."

Chapter 19 - The Tallest Free Standing Mountain in the World - Going Down

We safely descended to Kibo Hut in less than an hour. (It took about four to get up). I changed clothes, took a nap and went back outside with my radio to try to contact the rest of the team. I also brought out a bottle of Coke I had carried with me from Wisconsin. I borrowed this tradition from Lou Whittaker on Mt. Rainer who also took a bottle of Coke to the tops of mountains where he opened it and drank it. Carbonated soda tastes pretty good after a climb; it helps clean out the junk in your mouth. I sat outside, ate cookies Connie had brought along, and enjoyed the Coke.

It was a quiet time at Kibo Hut camp with porters from all different climb teams lounging around taking it easy.

I started to track some team talk on the radio and butted in. By this time, all had reached Gilman's Point, the false summit and were on their way to Urhu Peak, the true summit at 19,340 feet. Corey was the first to arrive by more than an hour before the others, but soon, all were on top with hugs, photos and treats all around. And then, they started back down.

Corey came across a struggling climber from Denmark. The guy was lost and delirious. Corey no doubt saved this guy from some serious problems by helping, (dragging) him down most of the way to Kibo Hut.

One of the goof ups we made on final summit day was not taking enough drinking water along and everyone's tanks were on empty. True to his new nickname, "Lead Dog", Corey grabbed a bunch of Nalgene Bottles I had filled and headed back up the mountain to carry the water to the rest of our team. Corey also had a guide hold his camcorder while he made a neat speech at the summit. During the writing of this chapter Corey said, "I wish we could have got my Dad up here, I still think about it and what it would take to get him back over there and get him to the top."

Tom says, "Descending from Urhu Peak was a piece of cake until we had to climb back up occasionally to be able to descend further. Going down the scree was really fun. We were delighted, exhausted, and running out of water. Chad's knees and ankles were killing him and the rest of us were getting dehydrated. We had made another mistake by not taking more water with us – but we were told to carry as little weight as we could on the day of attempting the summit. That reduction in weight should not have included water."

One by one the team came back to Kibo Hut. They were greeted with orange drink from our porters and hugs from me now the official picture taker and water bottle filler.

We took about a two-hour rest to eat, change and get ready to descend back to Horombu Hut before it got dark. Madeline accepted, (not too willingly) a bag of IV fluids to ward off dehydration effects, and Connie tried to sleep away a headache she got on the mountain.

Tom says, "Our entire team (except Corey) was exhausted but we realized that we needed to descend even further to Horombo Hut before we could call it quits for the day. Jeff was off on the beast like a shot and the rest of us were now just "running on adrenaline". I don't know how Chad made it with his bum knees and ankles and Madeline was still feeling terrible. Bryon was getting ornery for the first time and my body was running out of juice. We had been climbing and descending for about 18 hours now."

A high point of this day was my opportunity to fly down the trail on my own. Bryson was nervous about letting me go, (he really became part of our team) but eventually he admonished me to be careful and away I went. I kept my speed at about 20 mph and reached the rocky start of the descent in less than an hour. The rest of the team spread out behind, many walking alone, lost in their own thoughts about what they had accomplished.

When I got to the rocky section, I kept going, having fun trying to maneuver around all the rocks. I finally got to a point where I felt I should wait for the others. But, a couple of porters came by and motioned to me that they would help me move ahead, so I went with them. Danged if I did not get on a steep side slope and tipped the Beast over. As I rolled in the ditch, the porters looked on in horror but quickly got me upright and back on the trail. I maybe went another few hundred yards, before some of my team caught up with me.

Most of us reached Horombu in the daylight, but Chad, Bryan and Madeline came in just after dark, just before we were going to start worrying about them in earnest. As a team together most of the time, this was a time, where many of us appreciated the opportunity to be by ourselves for a while.

Dinner this night was accompanied by beer…hmmm, it tasted pretty good. And, bedtime came early, as we had been up a long, long time.

October 1st, Wednesday today, would be another long one, but we hoped, easier, for it was all downhill. Our reward would be hot showers, more beer and a nice bed. My cold had gone to my head and combined with altitude, I was plugged up and the farther I went down the mountain, the less I could hear and the larger my head felt. Poor Corey, he was coughing steadily, together we were not exactly an advertisement for healthy outdoor living! Connie says, "As I slept among the bedbugs and ate Zebra for dinner, I felt like one of the luckiest people in the world."

I was on the Beast and going down was about as body busting as going up. Every time I dropped into a ditch, it was bone jarring and dusty. I could not hear very well, and had no success in trying to equalize the air pressure between my ears. There was not much of the trail I could do on my own. I had Corey in the front, and usually Tom and Chad on each rear wheel. Corey would yank me out of the ditches, and Tom and Chad would hold me back as I slid into them. There was just nothing very easy about this mountain for sure.

We had lunch at Mandara Hut; I just sprawled on the ground while the others went inside for food. Kristin gave me some hot tea, which really hit the spot. I also ate some chicken, which I think was undercooked, but it tasted good.

After lunch, we kept descending and finally reached the porter road, which we took instead of the hiker path. Finally, I was able to go on my own for the last 3 miles. Even though my head was getting worse, it was great fun to glide down the road, up and over swells and ruts and be by myself for a while.

Tom says, "the descent was certainly easier than the climb but the rocks, roots, drainage ditches, and everything else we encountered on the way up were still there on the way down. This time Chad and I had to pull back on Jeff's bike to keep him from bouncing through the rough terrain rather that pull up – which was the endless case on way up. I looked at Jeff eating the dust that we were raising on the way down and began to realize what an unbelievable pounding this must be on his body – a major part of which he had no idea what effect it was happening. I just hoped that we were not doing some damage to him."

At one point, something crossed the road in front of me, as I got closer, I could see it was a large monkey...I am not sure who was more surprised by the other creature. I pulled up at a picnic table to wait for the rest of the team to catch. Once again, I tried to hold my nose and blow to equalize the pressure in my head. And, POW, I had a painful escape of air out my good ear. The pressure went down a bit, but the pain of the pop was bad and when I swallowed, I could feel a crinkling in my head like all the little ear bones had cracked in pieces. Connie says, "It was humbling. It was painful. It was spiritual. It was peaceful. I've never had a better time in my life."

We soon arrived at the Mandara Gate and the official end of the climb. We took the obligatory photos of the finish sign with us grouped around, did some paperwork and then loaded into vehicles to drive to the hotel. Well, I did not get out of the Beast. Since it was downhill to the hotel on a blacktop road, I stayed on the bike and followed the vehicles down. It was like in a parade. Kids were just getting out of school, elders walking to and from places and me. People were clapping and yelling at me as I flew down the hill. Jambo here and Jambo there, and despite feeling physically pretty bad, it was great fun to cruise that last mile or so and interact with the Africans. Again, what a gracious and friendly people.

Back at the hotel, the team and our porters got together on a large covered porch for a few rounds of beers, photos and handshakes. Tom, our ever-organized quartermaster oversaw the distribution of gear to the porters as part of the show of appreciation for all they have done for us. JanSport provided heavy hooded sweatshirts, Polarmax provided two different shirt tops, one light and one heavy and Granite Gear provided very warm hats. We took photos of them in their new clothes and at one point they all rose up and sang us a song. It was pretty neat and Connie captured it all on videotape.

At supper that night, we agreed to hang around one day to organize our gear, write postcards and generally relax before heading out on safari. I headed off to bed, while the others continued to celebrate.

October 2nd, Thursday I woke up even sicker than before, I was really getting dehydrated, coughing bad, now nausea, and a rising temperature. Bryan and Madeline started an IV and did what they could to make me comfortable and my roommate, Corey did even more to help out. I was just not getting better. At one point, I drank an entire Nalgene bottle of Endourox to try to regain some fluids, well, it only took about 20 minutes and it all came back up again. I had been also taking Darvacet, which is a narcotic painkiller, and now I was starting to get strange dreams when I closed my eyes. They were not scary, but for a person who normally does not dream, it was strange.

I lay in bed all day without getting any better. Several times, hotel staff visited me with hot tea and toast, which I tried to drink and eat, but with little success.

About 10:00 p.m. that night, Bryan made the call to get me into the local hospital. He felt it was necessary to do that to stop the dehydration process. It was a short drive to the hospital and a nurse who took me to the room I would stay in met us. It had two beds, bars of the window and a door to the toilet that was shared by an adjoining room. The odor of disinfectant was overwhelming. Once in bed, a Doctor and nurse checked me. They took my blood pressure with an old mercury type device and measured by temperature with an old thermometer in the mouth. They took a blood sample for malaria testing and started another IV. The trick that worked was an injection of a medication to lessen the nausea symptoms. Once the injection started to work, I experienced a huge sweat and a thirst, which was welcome. While the nausea was held at bay, I drank lots of water and juices and then fell asleep. I had several injections during the night and next morning. Chad pulled guard duty and stayed with me until morning, when Corey took over.

Tom says, "I know that Jeff was in bad shape and I was scared. He looked terrible and sounded worse. The idea that he was going to a hospital in Africa was frightening enough. I was worried whether or not he was going to make it. Kristin consoled me and tried her best to assure me that he would be ok – but I was scared shitless for him and not much else entered my mind except to pray that somehow, he could recover – and as usual, the son-of-a-bitch did. He is a remarkable person and I love him dearly, but he still drives me nuts once in a while."

October 3rd, Friday In mid-morning, three doctors visited me. An African, (the one from the night before,) a German and a Norwegian. The Norwegian Doctor had been in Tanzania for quite awhile and the German was his replacement. After a very thorough examination, the Norwegian Doctor recommended that I stay in that hospital bed for about a week before attempting to fly home. Most of my team was in the room at that pronouncement and we all looked at each other with very wide eyes. As soon as the Doctors left the room, we made plans for my escape. While Bryan went to process the formal paperwork for my discharge, the rest of us worked to get me ready to go back to the hotel. This all took about an hour and soon I was safely back in my bed at the hotel still with an IV and still needing the nausea shots which Madeline painlessly gave to me. Bryan settled with the hospital for my stay. The total bill came to $13.00 in USA dollars. There was a sign at the cashier's office of the hospital that listed the costs for certain medical procedures. A C-section was top on the list at $20.00. Delivering a baby the normal way was $9.00; a broken limb was $7.00 and snakebite was a real bargain at $2.50.

I could tell I was getting better, but still in no condition to do anything but lay in bed, which is what I did. We had to postpone the Safari one day, but the goal was to leave tomorrow. I did not want to be the continuing problem and wanted dearly to be better by morning. Corey figured a way to snake the Sat Phone from outside into our room so I could talk to Jane. She was very worried that I was taken to a hospital and wanted to hear my voice to reassure herself that I was doing ok. It was good medicine to hear her voice.

That night Corey went beyond the call of normal duty of taking care of his sick Father. Several days of strange medications, hit and miss food, and a return from dehydration all played a part in a bad onset of diarrhea. And,

supposed to do it. Slow, methodical, well hydrated and well energized. If you want to know how to climb this mountain, ask Connie.

I thanked Kristin for also her quiet determination to do whatever the rest of us asked of her. Her back and arm massages surely contributed to our success. She also obtained free of charge the use of the Satellite Phone we all relied on to talk with family back home. Kristin, (Angel Hands) has become a dear family friend of ours over the years. She was our lead guide on our successful trip up Norway's Mt. Galdopiggen in 2000 and she also was with our family when I endured the brain tumor surgery later that fall.

I thanked Tom, (Chinook) for all his excellent work as Quartermaster. (If you ever take a trip like this, make sure somebody knows where everything is!) Tom also was a mainstay on my struggle up and down the mountain. I hope his back and feet return to normal after hefting and heaving me over rocks, trenches and whatever else got in our way.

I thanked Chad, (Charging Spirit) for all he had done on my left side doing the same thing Tom was doing on the right. Chad, before the climb quietly raised a significant amount of money to pay for the team costs on the climb. His company, Adventis, was a big supporter of what we do. Chad has been on every one of my climbs and has carried me on his back more times than he cares to remember. During my night in the Marango Hospital, Chad stood guard, swatting mosquitoes and making sure I was still breathing. I know in his heart, he wanted me on top of that mountain, maybe more than I did.

And Corey, what more can I say about the Lead Dog? Corey had to miss one of our climbs, and I think he regrets that to this day. This man, not only carried me up the mountain while in my chair, (he had to lift me blindly over rocks and ditches) but also led the way back down. He was a blur of motion, tossing rocks out of the way, pulling on the tether, and slowing me down from behind. He was also our team cyber space whiz, by figuring out how to use the Satellite Phone and the Capricorn's ancient computer. Before and after the climb, Corey was also our WEB master contact.

When I was sick at the hotel, Corey went beyond the call of duty in taking care of me. For that, I owe him dearly.

I did not know it in Arusha, but when Corey was alone at the Kili Summit, he made a beautiful video tape with a message for me and his wife and little girl. My wife, Jane, and I still get misty eyed when we watch it.

While the others went shopping, I hung out with Sammy near the cars. We were continually hounded by young salesmen wanting to sell us anything from trinkets, to paintings to flags to jewelry. One guy told me he had just returned from a mine, and had a rare piece of Tanzanite that he would sell me at a huge discount. I asked him about mining, and how he got there, and why he was so clean looking after being in a mine. He could tell I would be a hard sell. I let it be known to the group of sales guys that I wanted a Tanzanian flag. All they could find were very small patches, which I did not want. Then they offered to climb the flagpole in front of the United Nations complex and steal the flag if I would pay them $150. I declined.

As we neared the airport for our long flight home, we stopped at a plush motel complex of modernized Masia "huts". We had an opportunity to clean up and repack our gear before being hosted for yet another feast of wine and munchies. Jody Schuster of Borton Travel had set this up unbeknown to us and provided the African wine. The owner of the Capricorn toasted us and we exchanged pleasantries and learned more about the history of the area.

Tom says, "I really felt the owner of the Capricorn was looking for some investors to help him expand the structure. He was talking to the wrong bunch of people if that was the case because none of us was in a position to help him out financially. We had saved or scratched out the funds to make this wonderful experience a reality and were in no position to offer thousands of dollars to help him reach his goal."

Soon it was time to get to the airport, check in, say good-bye to our many new friends, endure security checks, cruise the airport gift shop and finally jump on the plane. We first went to the City of Darussalam to pick up other passengers and then finally headed north to Amsterdam. Corey and I continued to cough and the flight was packed so this time we did not have the luxury of spreading across several seats.

October 7th, Tuesday in Amsterdam we said our goodbye to Kristin. Connie did some video interviews and we all cruised the shops for last minute trinkets. Our plane was late getting into Detroit, (that usually happens when flying in from Europe) and we missed our flight to Green Bay. Madeline was so homesick to see her son, Anthony, she took a flight to Milwaukee where he was staying with relatives. The rest of us lounged around the airport until our late flight was finally called for boarding.

There was still a crowd waiting for us in Green Bay including some TV reporters. There were lots of hugs and hand shaking as we waited for our luggage. Soon we were home and telling story after story about our adventures.

Epilogue - As I write this draft in early January of 2004, I reflect that it has been a tough row to hoe since returning home. I had to enter the hospital for some back surgery and shortly after that went back in to treat an out of control blood infection. I still was not back to the physical shape I was in before the trip, but hopefully every day saw some improvement.

We all have spent time looking over and sorting photos and films from the trip. Connie produced at least two excellent TV reports that received airtime across the Country. Tom prepared an excellent Power Point presentation.

We have maintained contact with our new friends in Africa and sent medical equipment and supplies to the little hospital that took care of me in Marangu.

As I look back on the trip, it is the people that I will remember most. On our team, the cooperation and teamwork were the best I had ever experienced.

In addition, the Tanzanian people and their culture was something that still impresses me. They are warm, friendly and color blind. Some may say they are a third world country, but in many aspects, their culture is more advanced than ours.

The Outdoors is still a place I want to be. Are we going on another adventure? I don't know. All I do know is to **Never Say Never!**

Chapter 20 - The Right to Risk

The "Right to Risk" documentary was filmed in May 2005. A well-equipped film crew followed eight individuals with significant physical disabilities on a 15-day whitewater raft trip. The plan was to float, row and paddle down 225 miles of Colorado River through the most inaccessible and awe-inspiring environment of Arizona's Grand Canyon. I was one of the chosen eight.

To have the right to take a chance or to make a decision is often something that people with disabilities never have. This film was all about taking chances and making decisions on our own behalf. The theory behind the documentary and the message was sound even if in reality the trip for me was not all that risky or eye awakening.

You may have heard of the saying, "It's not what you know but who you know". And that was the case here. I had met folks from the Phoenix area through Ski for Light and had been to Phoenix to teach sled hockey. When the opportunity came up to participate in this adventure, I admit that it sure helped having contacts with the City of Phoenix. Not only did I get to take a three week rafting trip I was also in on the pre-event projects like scouting the river ahead of time, selecting the candidates to raft and work on specialized gear that would help disabled people deal with life in a most inhospitable place.

With only one opportunity to capture the events of the trip, the trip organizers packed a large amount of video and audio gear: two large cameras, three small cameras, waterproof microphones, transmitters, batteries, chargers, generators and anything else they might need.

Managing the hot sun, cold water, windstorms, and whitewater in the Grand Canyon was only the first major challenge. The following year the team edited the 60 hours of footage into a 57-minute documentary for public television. Their film "Right to Risk" is a testament to the power of people with disabilities to be active participants in our society and independent in their own lives.

The actual trip started on May 12, 2005 when we pulled up to the beach at Lee's Ferry, ten miles below Glen Canyon Dam. Professional River guides were preparing the five oar boats and two motor rigs. We were 36 people, scheduled to raft through some of the most exciting rapids and spectacular scenery in North America. We would take all the food, water, camping and, medical, equipment we would need for the whole trip, as there were limited opportunities to resupply.

Interestingly, we would take all of our poop out with us. 36 people times 15 days -- the calculation was intimidating. Moreover, while we are talking about it, urination was only allowed in the river or to be dumped into the river after peeing into a bottle. The area is so hot and dry, the stench from urine and feces of thousands of annual visitors on land would be intolerable. Going in the river falls under the environmental rule, "the solution to pollution is dilution." You might also be slightly interested to know I never saw a naked butt during the entire trip. Modesty and respectfulness prevailed at all times.

It was a diverse crew. Eight severely disabled adults. Eleven staff and volunteers to support them. Nine river guides. And eight people on the video team.

Let me introduce you to the disabled group: Kathy and Sebastian are both totally blind; Sebastian is also deaf in one ear, like me. Josh has cerebral palsy, but was a highly ranked disabled downhill skier.. Judith has multiple sclerosis, and a limited ability to walk. Daniel is a "Lost Boy" from Sudan who has no use of his legs since a botched surgery by a missionary doctor in Kenya. Teresa, a diabetic has one crippled leg and one artificial leg and gets around on arm crutches. Susan suffered a horrible stroke at age 21, which left her without the use of arms, legs, voice. She went on to get doctorate in microbiology and studies anthrax for the Department of Defense.

In the beginning, the 36 people meshed pretty well, but by the end of the trip rough spots started to erupt and for most it was time to go home. However, you will not see that in the video.

There's a difference between the oar boat experience and the motor rig. The river guide skillfully steers, with very long oars, an inflated raft along with the current. The raft usually carries four passengers and almost all their gear and food and drinking water. On the oar raft, one is very much in tune with the flow of the river and the rhythms of nature. My favorite part of running rapids was the moments of quiet in the headwater before slipping into the froth.

The motor rig is a much larger raft powered by a 50 horse Honda outboard motor. This boat is a better bet through a rapid, but a less satisfying direct experience. We had two of them to meet the needs of medical and support equipment. The entire group switched often between the rafts and even smaller two or one-person inflatable kayaks called "duckies".

Having sorted and loaded an incredible amount of food and equipment, we strapped on our life vests, pushed off from shore, and set off. Surprisingly, we settled into a routine fairly quickly. Find a nice beach, anchor the boats, set up the disabled loo (a portable toilet in a tent), and eat lunch. Then back on the river, through a few rapids, and look for a place to camp.

When we landed for the night, the first chore was to unload the boats. This can take up to 30 minutes and involve a line of 20 of us passing gear hand to hand. Almost everyone participated in the line no matter the disability. Those not on the line began setting up tents, cots, chairs and other gear.

One of the more complicated tasks in setting up camp was putting together the cots, which consisted of sliding metal tubes until they popped in place and then arranging the support structures. There were about 20 cots to assemble every night. Sebastian, the blind guy quickly mastered the assembly of these cots and made quick work of it. I was impressed with his ability to do this hands on job and also with his ability to play poker as he did win a bit of money off of me during the trip.

We ate like kings and queens. We had salmon, chicken, steak, lasagna, pork chops, chili, salad, dessert and vegetarian selections. And, if you wanted, there were seconds at every meal. Some of us lived and slept in tents while others just slept on cots under the stars. Most of the guides slept on the rafts themselves, lulled to sleep with the gentle wash of the river currents.

We woke to the cry of "Cofffeee!" around 5:30 each morning. While others devoured huge breakfast of eggs, bacon or ham, fruit or French toast, I did my repacking and bathroom chores. If I was done early I often casted for fish, wrote in my diary or read a book. On several nights, they made a delicious pre dinner snack of the trout I had caught. One thing I enjoyed was that we didn't rush; we stayed on "river time."

A morning meeting was held each day, to attend to logistics. Josh liked to lead many of those meetings with a combination of humor and enthusiasm. His vigor for living infused the whole campsite. Born with cerebral palsy, his speech is slurred, but full. His body is subject to tremors, which means he will ask you to make his sandwich or pour his coffee. His spirit is indomitable. "It's going to be another beautiful and wonderful day, and we're all going to have the best time ever. But, first, it's come to my attention that someone has placed toilet paper in the pee bucket in the tented loo. Please, put the toilet paper in the biohazard box. Now, Kathy is going to lead us in stretches, Scott and Jeff are going to lead us in Tai Chi, and Teresa will read something inspirational."

Carol Gary, from Phoenix Park and Rec would read the boat assignments and trip leader, Kyle George, youngest of the 36, would outline the day's itinerary ("down river, subject to change.") River guides would close the kitchen. Camera crews would wrap the morning shooting, last call for the loo, and we were back on the river.

If they could choose, all eight of the disabled folks would be on the oar boats all the time, even through the dread and famous rapids with names like Sockdologer, Granite, Hermit, Crystal, and, especially, the mother of them all, Lava Falls. It was only Lava that the staff kept Susan off. If Susan fell in the water, she could not hold her breath or hold her head up. She was bummed to be on a motor rig through the Canyon's greatest ride, but rode out every other rapid in the bow of an oar boat, one supporter on each side of her, her face into the wash of white water, her spirit crying out "Here I am; bring it on!" No one ever lived more fully.

To communicate with Susan, you simply talk to her. She responds by pointing, slowly, to words and letters on a laminated word board. I thought this would take forever. However, her combination of intelligence and getting to the point helps you to finish each word she begins, and the conversation is easier than you'd think.

One day, we encountered a huge windstorm, so strong that it drove the oar boats upstream, against the Colorado's forceful current. Only with great effort could the rowers force the boats downstream. We pitched tents in the driving wind, some blowing away before we could anchor them, and settled in. I remember sitting in my tent in the dark holding on to the poles to keep it from blowing away, the dust was choking me. The next morning was calm but me and all my gear was covered with about a half inch of sand flour dust.

The first hike up a side canyon was Blacktail and we set out in the high heat of midday. The temperature was well over 100 degrees, the beginning of the hike steep, sandy and difficult. When we entered the slot canyon, the temperature dropped about 30 degrees. The hike ended at the very end, where the trail ends at a sheer wall, and water slides down the surface like a fountain in a corporate lobby (but better.) The pool here was clear water and warm which was a far cry from the muddy and very cold Colorado River. It was a great bath and I spent the better part of an hour soaking.

The next side canyon we visited was a short walk up Deer Creek to a driving waterfall. Wheelchairs were outfitted with aluminum poles, and four people could carry a passenger, sedan chair style. I liked the image of Daniel Deng, from the Dinka tribe in southern Sudan, carried by four white men -- the converse of images from childhood movies set in Africa; Daniel was fascinated hearing about them. The trail was sufficiently rocky and uneven that it was easier to carry the sedan chairs in the knee-deep creek. Too keep cool and for the fun of it, I lay in the creek and dog paddled down to the rafts rather than the sedan chair. I sort of felt like a spawning salmon going backwards.

A day later, we dawdled at a particularly great campsite, and Anne who was one of the able-bodied trip leaders from Phoenix organized a "sharing circle." We were half way through the trip, had gotten to know each other pretty darned well, the distinctions among the four groups were withering away, and now we were going to share whatever we wanted. Josh was handed the sharing stone and went first; he explained that he had never properly grieved his dad's death and that the watery wall at the end of the slot canyon had brought him face to face with his loss, but in a wonderful and fulfilling way. Everyone joined his crying. And on it went, for at least a couple hours, while the videographers taped it all. Great revelations, confessions, gratitude, exuberance, consolation -- and more tears. My god, those with severe disabilities had a lot to bear, but none of them complained or griped about that. They just spoke of what their lives were like. When my turn came, I held the stone and spoke about the magic of the outdoors and how it improved my life physically, mentally and socially. I told the group that the outdoors was my church and they were welcome to join.

When it came to the video crew to speak, Katrina, the producer, took the camera while another cameraman commented that "the very astute among you have probably noticed that Andy and I share a disability -- it's called 'each other.' But we're learning from you how to cope. We take no pleasure in sticking our lenses and our microphones in your faces at intimate moments, but it's what we have to do to tell this story, so please trust and forgive us." Thirty-six very diverse people had something to say, and everyone benefited greatly from what everyone else said.

As luck would have it, one of the main cameras broke and was unrepairable. One of the cameramen, Dave, it turned out, was down by the river receiving a new camera body from San Anselmo. Despite the implausibility of resupply on the river, Dave had used the trip's satellite phone to call Eli Adler, owner of the broken camera, and asked him to replace it. Eli flew a new camera to Flagstaff; a river guide picked it up at the airport and drove it to the South Rim, where it was placed on a mule at 3:00 am. The mule lugged it down to Phantom Ranch, a mile from the river. A passing motor rig from Arizona River Runners picked it up and brought it downstream until they saw our boats. Delivery time from San Anselmo to the sharing circle: about 20 hours. FedEx, eat yer heart out! And, Dave sent the broken camera on down river.

A day on the river can be a day to remember forever. Fifteen days on the river is like a special treat from Mother Earth. I calculated that any quarter mile section of the Canyon could stand alone anywhere in the country, and draw visitors from everywhere. In 225 miles, there were 900 such quarter miles: steep canyon walls, waterfalls, rock falls, side canyons, cactus, bighorn sheep, reflections, eddies, every kind of rock the earth has tossed up in the last two billion years (take a few million or so), fossils, and fantastic arrays of clouds and sunsets, and moonrises, and stars. The oar boat is silent, it flows with the river current, and every bend in the river offers another spectacular view.

Kyle, the trip leader, made a welcome decision when he decided we would camp at National Canyon for three whole nights, our only "stay over." We camped river left on a broad open space, with both sandy and non-sandy campsites. Stu, our E.R. doc, played and sang the blues. Josh hiked up to the end of National Canyon; a walk he said took about 45 minutes. I of course fished. Susan and Daniel swam - Daniel's first swim since he swam from Sudan to Ethiopia ten years ago, dodging the bullets of soldiers, and losing hundreds or thousands of Lost Boys and Girls in a single massacre.

The two video crews, and Katrina, conducted personal interviews. Lance, a Hopi Indian, explored. We all napped in the shade during the heat of the afternoon. Most of the disabled interviews where what you expected in such a place. The common descriptions used were, "life changing, amazing, never was able to do anything like this, I am a new person blah, blah, blah." When the interviewer asked me if the trip had changed me I had to say no much to their surprise. The reason I said no was that this trip was like so many of my other adventures in the outdoors. I had experienced the great feelings before, was doing it again and plan to do it in the future. I guess most of the other disabled rafters figured this would be it, their first, last and only great outdoor adventure.

The next day, we set out for the end of National Canyon. Josh, the guy who had cerebral palsy, had done it in 45 minutes the day before, but he hadn't adequately described the two rock falls he had crossed. No paths, it took eight people to carry me, in a sedan chair, over the huge boulders, a team of four passing me up to the next team of four. Then the same workers (staff, volunteers, river guides, even video crew) would double back for the next sedan chair. Sebastian and Kathy each followed a guide, walking every step of the way. I was amiable in my sedan chair, but asked not to be photographed in it unless my wheels were on. I didn't mind the help, but I didn't want to appear that helpless – because I am not. It did not take long for the sedan carriers to realize that having the wheels left on the chairs actually made the task easier.

Chapter 20 - The Right to Risk

We finally arrived at the end, where the canyon narrows to two rock walls, about three feet apart, with a small waterfall cascading between them. The only way to continue is to "chimney" up the walls, with one's back pressed against one wall and feet pressed against the other. Kathy, the blind girl was guided up the narrow passage to the pristine spa at the top. She was elated.

The last afternoon on the river, Kathleen Jo, the project director insisted that two videographers take a turn in an oar boat. They tried to decline, as they couldn't shoot from one, because the gear would certainly get wet. But they took the offer and boarded Faye's boat, with Lance, the Hopi Indian and myself. Daniel Deng was in the front of a "rubber ducky," an inflatable kayak, with one of the volunteers, Sandy, in the rear of the ducky. They paddled safely through Rapid 205 and headed downstream for 209. Faye shouted at them, "There's a huge hole on the right; paddle hard to stay to the left!"

As Faye negotiated our way through 209, I looked down into the hole and gulped. It looked mean and deep. As soon as we were through, I watched Daniel and Sandy, and watched helplessly as they disappeared into the hole. We really didn't know if Daniel would make it. Faye sounded an emergency warning to the motor rig downstream, and maneuvered us into a rescue position. It seemed forever before I saw Daniel's two thin arms stretched skyward, and I became hopeful. The motor rig passed us -- and Daniel. We had exactly one shot at saving him. The videographers were in the bow, Lance and I in the stern. Faye put the boat right in his path, and Lance grabbed him. I helped Lance land him upright in the boat, both of us ready to force the water out of him. Daniel sputtered, spit, and finally smiled. He said, "I could not allow myself to die in the Colorado River."

There were three estimates of how long Daniel was in the water. I said five minutes. Faye said 90 seconds. Daniel said about one hour. We were each totally sincere. Daniel had become the first Dinka to swim a rapid in the Colorado River. And the river gods rewarded Lance, a day later, when his lost $500 prescription sunglasses appeared in the bottom of the oar boat.

That night was our last, and familial, together. We sang, toasted, told true stories and tall tales, laughed, cried and hugged. We had started out as four distinct units and had melded gradually into a homogeneous group. What had seemed to me, at the beginning, a nearly impossible and very lengthy and arduous journey, had suddenly ended, and now seemed too short, even too easy.

One of the videographers said, "I cannot overstate the awe and respect I have for the eight brave people who chose the "Right to Risk." They would not allow their disabilities to prevent them from exploring, enjoying, and exulting in one of the world's great rides. I am in equal awe of the compassionate staff and volunteers who worked as hard as people can work and loved every minute of it. And Mother Nature bless the river guides. Row all day, set up camp, cook dinner, AND provide tender and loving care to those who are less able." River guide Steve said to the participants. "You have inspired me. And you have provided fodder for my cannon the next time someone complains about something trivial."

Dr. Stu's medical evaluation: "No one died."

Two years later, I did the entire trip again. This time with four wheelchair users from Great Britain. I was again along to help them enjoy and manage the trip. I became the chief dishwasher and pan scrubber to help pay my way. Both were great adventures.

Chapter 21 - The Unfinished Business of Climbing Mount Boss

In July of 1995, I tried to get to the top of 14,173 foot Mt. Bross located about 20 miles south of Breckenridge, Colorado. Just a rookie mountain climber back then, I challenged the mountain in my every day sports chair. What a rude awakening! I made it about 3 yards before realizing I was going nowhere without some help from the rest of my friends that came along.

Who wins a race with a mountain? If you climb to the top, do you win? If you don't quite make it to the top, do you lose? If someone helps you get up the steep parts, does that break the rules and are you disqualified? The answers to those questions in order are, no one, not really, nope and nope.

Colorado has over 50 mountain tops called "Fourteeners" and it is a goal of many to climb as many of them as they can in their lifetime.

For me, (a self described "flat lander" from Wisconsin) just getting to the top of one of the "Fourteeners" would be good enough. I actually made it to the top of 14,090 foot Mt. Evans in 2005 too, but that is another story.

We ten would be climbers had all arranged to be in Winter Park, Colorado to make sure two of them were going to get married just like the wedding invitation said they were. (Scott Bertrand and Brenda Driscoll) Little Haley Wangberg and her brother Blake fitted nicely into Mom's, (Lisa) and Dad's,

(Jerry) backpacks. Big Dave Rowan from Seattle and his wife Nancy, (the oyster suppliers) and wife Jane and I made up the assault party.

The idea was simple enough. After the wedding, Scott and Brenda would postpone the honeymoon to make the climb. So, after the gifts were opened and the good byes waved at visiting relatives, our rag tag band traveled south of Breckenridge to the foot of Mt. Bross. A four-wheel drive was used to get to the tree line of the famous more than 2,000 year old Bristlecone Pines. I, anxious to get going and get away from the hoards of mosquitoes, started pushing up the trail in my every day wheelchair. Even with knobby tires, it became real apparent that I was not going anywhere in the direction of up without some help.

With the help of some ski poles and trial and error rope tying and teamwork, a mule team was fashioned from the strongest in the group, Dave, Jerry and Scott. With those three leading and either Nancy, Lisa or Jane pushing me, some progress was made usually in hard fought 100 yard increments.

The trail was a switchback that kept offering stupendous views, (normally reserved for those in airplanes) of other mountains and valleys. The higher our group climbed the thinner the air, the stronger the wind, and the more frequent encounters with snow. In fact at about 11,500 and more than 3 hours of steady work, it looked like the end of the climb was at hand. The trail was gone, hidden by large expanses of steep, slippery icy snow. After a quick lunch of peanut butter and pretzels that materialized out of Scott's backpack, a different route was planned to try and reach the summit. Another 400 feet of elevation was picked up and the top seemed so close, we thought we could taste victory.

Once the trail was abandoned, it became really apparent that this was no place for a wheelchair, so out came butt protector and the backward push-ups began with progress now measured in about 10 inch increments. Butting up 10 feet came at great expenses of lung and arm power. Butting up for another 100 feet finally registered with the brain that this could not go on. According to the altimeter we were resting for the umpteenth time at 12,000 feet and the top seemed like a stone's throw away, but it wasn't. Several of those with functioning legs took one last shot, (the weather was closing in quickly) but without success. Slippery snow covered rocks and high winds kept the summit an uninhabitable place for all on this day.

I was excited about the prospect of at least going back down un-assisted. But I was again in store for a rude awakening. Going downhill on this mountain in a wheelchair was almost as bad as going up. The "mule team" worked in reverse to slow the descent...but several times the chair choose to obey the laws of gravity rather than the human masters and broke free to crash and burn a few yards down the trail with me adding a few more wounds to a beat up body.

After six hours on the Mountain, the trip was over...who won? We guess that everyone did. A quote often used by famous Mt. Rainier mountain guide, Lou Whittaker and attributed to William O. Douglas is, "that the struggle of man against man produces jealousy, deceit, frustration, bitterness and hate. But, the struggle of man against the mountains is different. Man then bows before something that is bigger than he. And, when he does that, he finds serenity, humility and dignity."

As the beer came out of the coolers and the conversations waxed philosophical, I proposed as sort of a toast out loud, that the opportunity to compete in two Paralympics was a great experience...but William O. Douglas was right on the mark. There certainly would be less strife and trouble in the world if we all tried to climb a mountain together instead of always competing against each other.

As our tired group loaded up for the ride home, I turned for one last look at Mt. Bross and with hand raised a promise was made...**I WILL BE BACK!**

As I went on to climb Mt. Rainier, Mt. Whitney in the USA, Mt. Galdhopiggen in Norway and Mt. Kilimanjaro in Africa during the next 9 years, it was always in the back of my mind to try again to get up Mt. Bross.

In October of 2004, I had a second opportunity to try and summit Mt. Bross. This time, I had a bigger bag of tools including the One-Off Mountain Climbing Hand Cycle, (Christened the Mountain Beast.) Circumstances of team availability and other reasons to be in Colorado lead to the October attempt.

This time, snow really did become an issue. Starting at about 11,100 feet, drifts of snow laid across the trail. In the early morning hours, the snow was frozen and the Mountain Beast easily rode over the snow banks. But as the sun rose and the temperature reached melting, the snow turned soft and the bike wheels sunk more and more. But, with a harness of team members, I was still able to make upward progress. As the day wore on, the weather turned stormy and more snow began to fall and the wind picked up.

My team had reached about 13,600 feet and only about ¾ mile of trail to the top. But, rounding a corner brought the full fury of the storm and once again we had to retreat in the face of 3-4 foot snow depths and winds exceeding 40 mph.

Fast Forward to August/September, 2005. To say getting to the top of Mt. Bross was becoming as obsession might be going too far, but I decided to try one more time to get to the top and to set some personal rules for getting there.

First, the other two tries involved support team pulling and pushing. I, while appreciative of the teamwork, wanted to try and summit under my own power and accepting help only when no other alternatives were available. Also, the other two attempts were one-day shots starting at tree line at about 11,000 feet. I determined to do it alone. I would need at least three days and I wanted to start well below tree line at the little old mining town of Alma. The total climb would exceed 12 miles.

DAY ONE: Alma to Base Camp at Windy Ridge. This segment involved hand cycling a gravel and rock road from 9,250 feet to 11,339 feet. The distance was 5.3 miles and took me 3 ½ hours. I was dropped off in Alma while the rest of the team drove to Windy Ridge to set up camp. From my Diary: "As I started up the road, several trucks and cars passed me. I am sure the drivers wondered just what the heck I was up to. Much of the road paralleled a mountain stream and the gurgling of water pouring over rocks was welcome background music. "

"The blue sky was starting to cloud up and I heard claps of thunder. But, from t-shirt weather, instead of rain, a splattering of wet snow started falling. About an hour into the ride, my son Corey came zooming down the road on his mountain bike. The others had found the campsite and had almost finished setting up base camp. "

"Dinner was ready when I finally peddled into camp. Wet and cold, I quickly changed into warm clothes, enjoyed a great meal, campfire, stargazing and conversation. Sleep came quickly."

DAY TWO: Windy Ridge to Dolly Varden Mining Camp Ruins. This segment involved hand cycling from 11,339 feet to 13,115 feet. The distance was 4.8 miles and lasted 6 hours going up and 45 minutes to descend back to base camp. From my Diary: "There seemed to be no need to start real early, so I slept in and actually got on my bike about 9:00 am. The rest of the team also started climbing and quickly left me to slowly move ahead at my own pace. My wife Jane who had been with me on the first attempt, 10 years ago, kept a steady pace and summited early in the afternoon with my Daughter in Law, Sara."

"As I picked my way over the rocky trail I with some regularity would loose traction and slide backward several feet until my drive tire found purchase. At one point, the rocks on the road became so bad, I tried to move hard left off the road to where the surface seemed a bit less challenging. I managed to get stuck sideways and while rocking the Mountain Beast back and forth did a very nice tumble and ended up on my back with the Beast on top. "

My backpack hydration bladder, still with some water cushioned my fall and no damage was done. I was very glad to have a Talkabout radio along and gave a yell for help. Before some of my team descended to give me a hand, I

was able to at least unstrap myself from the bike and get in a sitting position. When my friends showed up, they helped me to get back in the saddle
and once again start moving upward. I finally moved past that very tough
100 yard stretch and again was on my own.

Thunderhead clouds began forming in mid-afternoon. Other team members
except for my Son had already headed to base camp. I was out of water and
beat. The ride back down to base camp was not a fun thing. The Beast has
no shocks and the ride was in a word, torturous."

DAY THREE: Dolly Varden Mining Camp Ruins to Summit. This segment involved hand cycling from 13,115 feet to 14,173 feet. The distance
was 2.1 miles and lasted 4 hours going up and 30 minutes back down to the
Mining Camp.

I was driven to the mining ruins in a 4WD truck to start the last day.
Original plans called for bivouacking at the mining camp ruins but the daily
threat of late afternoon lighting storms required getting off the mountain
and below tree line for safety reasons.

From My Diary: I was pretty stiff and sore from two solid days of hand
cycling at a snail's pace. We had risen before dawn and had reached the
mining camp just at sunrise. There was no wind and the day showed
promise of being just perfect. Soon, my muscles loosened up and I seemed
to be making decent progress. At some points, the trail was so steep, the
back drive tire just spun. But, Corey merely applied some downward

pressure on the frame and I was able to spin forward. About one hour into the climb, I had passed the turn-a-round point from last year. I felt good about at least surpassing my previous best on this mountain.

For whatever reasons, this part of the mountain seemed easier to negotiate. There were some tough spots, but for the most part I was moving right along. As I got higher and higher the view got better and better. I started to believe that finally I would get to the top and soon, there I was on top of the world in the crystal blue ski, warm temps and no wind.

One of the team, unknown to me, had lugged up a bottle of champagne. You know, it did not taste half bad! We stayed on the summit for about 40 minutes enjoying the view; camaraderie and sharing cell phone talk time with friends back home.

"It was time to start the descent back to the mining camp and our vehicle. The punishment my arms, chest and shoulders took on the way down was again much worse than on the way up and the two days of descending just about did me in. Finally getting back to camp, clean clothes, beer, huge steaks and another round of stargazing became a fitting end to another annual adventure of a lifetime."

Chapter 22 - Climbing Mt. Evans

Are you tired of competitive racing against others? Are you tired of losing? Are you tired of winning? How about moving up the competitive ladder and try to compete against yourself? These were the beginning words in a story I wrote for the premier wheelchair sports magazine called "SportsN'Spokes" in the fall of 2007. I was 58 years young.

I was in Colorado for a speaking engagement for the National Park and Recreation Association on disabled accessibility and the outdoors. I took advantage of a free airline ticket and speaker stipend to come early and stay later to visit friends and play outside in mountain country. I spent a few days near Winter Park with friends Chuck, Marie Huston, and Tim Byas. I borrowed a handcycle from the Winter Park Adaptive Recreation Program and Tim and I rode all around the back roads between Winter Park and Granby. It was great exercise at high altitude and helped acclimate me from the lower elevations in Wisconsin. Moreover, it was neat to be in a near wilderness setting. Tim has helped me for years as my right hand man at various Ski for Light events plus a rafting trip on the San Juan River in 2005. He has bailed me out of lots of "deep doo doo" situations and we have many memories to share.

After my speaking work was finished in Colorado Springs, I spent a day at Craig Spinal Cord Hospital in Denver. I visited with patients and staff and got to try a few modern hand bikes. I choose one to use the next day to try to get up Mt. Evans.

So, on the first of August 2007, four hand cyclists took a ride up Colorado's Mt. Evans. This 14,270' peak near Idaho Springs, boasts the highest black-top road in the USA. The road ends at 14,143'. From the parking lot at the bottom to the end of the road, it is 15 miles of switchback roadway, 99.99% is acutely uphill.

Starting at dawn, our small band of bikers, led by Coloradoans Drew Wills and Sherry Schulz, started moving up the road. Not long after, another athlete from Colorado, Steve Ackerman took off, and bringing up the rear was me, the self-described flatlander from Wisconsin. In the mix were about a dozen family members, friends and representatives of Craig Hospital. My support crew consisted of Tim, Marie, Kristin Johnson and Scott Bertrand all long time friends. The Craig Recreational Therapy folks are always looking for more ways to get patients to play outside and this certainly was outside in the mildly extreme.

A team approach to most outdoor adventures helps everyone get higher up the hill or deeper into the wilderness. However, this time most of the sweat and effort would be self centered. Further, the story that I wrote reminded readers that since at least the mid 1800's factual medical documentation can be found proving the value of the outdoors to improve physical, mental and social health. This is especially true for those of us with the label "disabled."

I purposely hung back until everyone else started out. I did not want to make a race out of this. With ancient competitive instincts still in the recesses of my brain, I knew if I saw another hand biker I would expend valuable energy trying to keep up. And that would have been futile with the other well adapted and top shape athletes on the road that day. (Sherry had just returned from Alaska after winning the 267-mile Sadler's Ultra Challenge Race.)

As with other climbs I have done, I tried to get in a zone of just moving upward enjoying the good exercise and the beauty of the outdoors. However, it was tough trying to find the zone when my breathing was almost redlining from the get go. It was cold at the start, but it wasn't long before I started shedding outerwear. I had a GPS strapped to my foot and an occasional glance at it showed I was usually staying over my objective of at least two miles an hour. Most of the time, I was in the lowest granny gear trying not to blow up aerobically but still maintaining headway. Experienced athletes recognize this as a "good burn" workout.

Although the road was black ice pavement, the camber made it difficult to steer the bike as it wanted to pull to one side or the other. This really made things tough as I had to sort of peddle sideways for long stretches of road. Hand cycles have camber adjustment calibrators, but I could not get mine to adjust properly. The fact that "I only ride them and not build them" worked against me once again! I usually don't but this time I did wear a small walkman with an ear bud in my good ear. I played about 100 songs during the climb, all designed to motivate me to keep plugging away.

Meanwhile, the other three hand bikers were "enjoying" similar experiences only at faster paces. Drew, in comparison to me was holding a 5 MPH average. The road was wide enough for cars to pass each other as well as bikers or hikers. Vehicle traffic became heavier as the day wore on, but most were either ambivalent or excited to see us climbing.

Back down were I was mightily trying to maintain a peaceful state of mental bliss, I did notice a change in the trees from tall evergreens to shorter trees and then at the tree line, the famous 1,000 year old Bristle Cone Pines. Then there were no trees and the view expanded ten fold. Wow, what a sight. Miles and miles of mountains, some still snow covered. Add to that, small lakes nestled in low spots down steep slopes below the road. I also came up close and personal to the Mountain's full time inhabitants - marmots, squirrels, mountain goats and sheep.

Drew reached the summit parking lot in just 3 hours. Steve was next and then Sherry. I enjoyed the rest stops on my way up to congratulate and chat with all of them as they made rapid descents back down the road.

The higher I went, the colder and windier it became. In addition, the higher I went the more frequent the rest stops. I was getting tired and my gas tank was nearing empty, but the parking lot was in sight and the excitement of nearing the goal was giving me a tiny bit of renewed energy. I made it to the top just after 6 hours of biking. After congratulations and photos at the summit it was my turn to rip down the mountain. I put warm clothes back on and what took over 6 hours to get up only took 55 minutes to get back down! I could of gone faster, but I rode the brakes much of the descent. I was well aware of the fact that most mountain climbing accidents happen on the decent and I did not want to become an accident statistic.

Later, over beers and French fries at an Idaho Springs pub, we all basked in what we all hoped would be just one more annual trip of a lifetime. Steve mentioned that he had lived in Colorado more that 35 years. Before he became disabled, he had hiked up Longs Peak. Since his accident, he has "climbed" most of Colorado's high mountain passes on his handcycle, but "bagging" another fourteener - Mt. Evans on a handcycle, was a new experience and something to do again on other mountains in Colorado.

I closed out the magazine story by telling the readers some succinct details about how to go to the next level of challenging themselves outside specifically here at Mt. Evans. I told them that Mt Evans is an Entry Fee National Park. The Federal Golden Access Passport is accepted. There are two restroom locations on the way up and one at the start and the top. All are accessible.

It is advisable to start your adventure very early in the day, as it is common for rain and thunderstorms to move in later in the afternoon. To help motorists to spot you, wear bright clothing.

The climb is not just for those with hand cycles. Any mobility aid wheelchair could also be used. Heck, I would challenge someone using crutches or a walker to take a chance. If you have the opportunity to be near Mt. Evans or any outdoor challenge, its OK if you don't make it to the goal/top on your first attempt or in many attempts. One interim goal to adopt is just try to go farther each time you go out. Like the title of this book shouts out...**Always Climb Higher!**

Chapter 23 - Quetico or How I Spend Father's Day

Every other Father's Day weekend, my sons, a climbing partner and I travel to Canada's Quetico Wilderness Area. Quetico is located just north of the United States and the state of Minnesota and is the Canadian version of the adjoining USA Boundary Waters.

The restrictions to use Quetico include no motorized watercraft, no metal cans or glass. There is no electricity or running water and no live bait or barbed hooks allowed for fishing.

For our June 2010 adventure, one of my sons needed to miss the trip so we filled in with another one of our climbing partners. After driving all night from Madison, Wisconsin we got a few hours' sleep in the vehicle before the registration station opened up. That did not take long and neither did packing the two canoes with all of our gear. We planned the trip to avoid portages but not long distances. Our destination was Roan Lake about 17 miles by water.

The Quetico is about 70% water and much of the 30% of land mass is in the form of hundreds of islands. It does not take much to get lost if you are not careful.

Other years the water at the embarking location was right up to the wooded shoreline. This year, due to years of low rain supply, the water was about 40 feet from shore. This made getting to the canoe with a wheelchair relatively easy. We spent the next five hours paddling to our destination on an island in Roan Lake. We choose an island because it was relatively easy to get to, it limited the possibility of bears scrounging for food at our site, and we could take advantage of more wind to keep the insect level low.

We took several breaks along the way. Around noon we enjoyed a shoreline lunch of venison sausage, Wisconsin cheese, crackers and candy bars. We have our own meaning for the word Quetico; we say it's the First Nation word for "the wind blows from different directions at the same time!" But today, the winds were calm, waves were nonexistent and the paddling easy.

We hoped to supplement the foods we packed with fish we caught, but for the first night our huge T-bone steaks had thawed nicely and were ready to grill on a grate over an aspen wood fueled fire.

Just as we finished eating a storm blew up and we retreated to the tents as sleep came easy after a long night of sitting in a car and then paddling. I brought my accessible tent from (Eureka from Blue Sky Design) and the other three slept in one large Yurt type tent. Since my tent had a vestibule, we all were able to sit inside nice and dry if a storm blew through.

We were to be gone from home for six days, the first and sixth where we drove and paddled to get to Roan Lake and back. The other four days were spent in a typical fashion of waking up, having a little brunch and heading out on the water for the day. The two canoes usually fished in different areas but we maintained contact with talk about radios. Since we had no refrigeration only fish that we wanted to eat that night were kept. The fish we did not keep for supper became memories with a digital camera. This year, the fishing was exceptionally good. We had no problem catching supper and more. Besides fishing we enjoyed the abundant wildlife with sightings of moose, otter, bald eagles, osprey, waterfowl and songbirds.

As I grow older I feel I am paying for my career as a world class disabled athlete (swimming & Nordic Skiing) with increasing aches and pains, stiffness and weaker muscles. Still, these trips are so enjoyable, we are considering making them annual lifetime adventures instead of every other year, not knowing how long I can continue to keep going.

What follows is the guts of this chapter which is a short encyclopedia of tips and tactics to take extreme outdoor adventures whether you are a young rookie or an aging wheelchair user.

First and foremost, these kinds of trips are partnerships with everyone pitching in to do what it takes to make things happen. As I get older and the physical skills diminish, I still do what I can. This includes the paperwork of applying for and obtaining entry permits, checking with customs about changing rules, (for example it was not legal to bring root crops like potatoes into Canada from the USA) and planning the menu including grocery shopping back home. I also plan the logistics of the drive to Canada and keep track of costs that we then split amongst us. My other chores included some cooking with the two gas stoves we brought along and cutting firewood.

In exchange, I need help getting to and from and in and out of the canoe. I also need help in erecting my tent and setting up some other gear. That help comes easy and readily. Disabled people should understand that when someone helps you to enjoy mutually likable adventures those giving the help usually get as much or more satisfaction as the person on the receiving end.

Do we "rough it"? Not really. I am able to pack in my canoe an accessible tent, a cot, warm sleeping bag, three-inch inflatable mattress and portable bathroom gear. I pack clothes sparsely consisting of a raincoat, short and long pants, two T-shirts, one long shirt and an extra pair of socks and underwear. While I am wearing some stuff, if needed, the other can be swished and dunked in the lake for a quick wash and dried in the canoe while paddling and fishing all day.

There are two top fears that play with a chair users mind, at least my mind! First is managing clean bathroom chores and second is getting dressed. I think the most valuable piece of equipment I have purchased over the years of wheelchair living is a portable toilet/shower chair. I never leave home overnight without it.

For wilderness trips I just take the seat and the four legs. I have plenty of privacy in the vestibule of my tent and an easy transfer from my cot to the seat. I never mastered pulling on my pants or a decent wash-up while sitting in my chair, thus the cot at wheelchair level is a godsend. I bring a supply of plastic bags and moist towelettes for waste and clean ups that get tossed with the used catheters into the campfire each night before turning in. For some reason, (knock on wood) I don't get many UTI's anymore, but I never travel without antibiotics just in case things start to go south.

Staying hydrated is always important. For our trips we bring small high-tech water filters to purify lake water and a bunch of plastic jars of Kool-aid and lemonade if we tire of drinking plain water. (By the way, one can get used to an evening cocktail consisting of warm alcohol of choice, coolish lake water and lemonade powder!)

In many stories on adventures, the authors often say "safety is the number one priority." Well, I could guess that some might say that just staying home would be the safest thing to do instead of opening one's self up to possible drowning, car crashes, insect bites, severe sunburn, bear attacks, getting lost or somehow otherwise injured.

We do think about safety too, but not necessarily the highest priority. Having a good first aid kit, GPS and maps, extra batteries, whistles, repair kits, duct tape, extra canoe paddles and walky-talky radios all are typical of the gear we bring with us. Maybe instead of being a number one priority, it's just second nature for us to expect the un-expected.

I can sit in a canoe all day either with a partner or alone. If there are 2 of us, I sit in the stern. I lowered the canoe seat almost to the bottom of the canoe to lower my center of gravity, help in balance and rest my arms on the gunnels. I also tilted the canoe seat backwards to help me stay seated and not slide out the front end. I top this arrangement off with a padded back/butt rest and a wheelchair cushion. If I am paddling alone, I move forward in the craft to a bit behind the center and sit on an extra cushion, the padded back/butt rest and then wheelchair cushion. My legs in both cases stretch out in front of me in a most relaxing fashion.

I bring a manual wheelchair for its lightness and hardiness. You won't spend much time getting around in the chair in this mostly aquatic environment, so even if you normally use a power or power assist chair, just bring a manual chair that others will help push and move into needed locations.

My son, two buddies and I must have been living right the past two years as the Quetico winds again stayed quiet on our last morning paddle out of the wilderness. We had a great bonfire last night disposing of the last of our dry goods, fire wood and other stuff we no longer needed for the trip out including the last of the booze but enough filled water bottles to last till we reached civilization.

I want to thank the good folks at Sports'n Spokes for encouraging me write this story. Remembering the good times is a very valuable commodity one can enjoy over and over again. Writing this and looking at the many pictures we all took gives me another chance to do just that!

Chapter 24 - Keep on Climbing - My Time at Rennes

In January 2011, I had the first of both shoulders replaced. I had to spend months in a rehabilitation/nursing home facility called Rennes. This chapter is comprised of a series of CarePage.com blogs. I wrote the blogs about being in Rennes during my first replacement rehabilitation.

I started by telling readers that: After over a year in hospitals and worse, I am in place to heal a badly damaged shoulder. The thought behind getting this shoulder replacement is we have 5 grandkids I would like to see grow up, a 50th wedding anniversary I would like to attend (Mine), a fishing boat that needs more use, a yet to be started book, and a unfinished obituary.

Why am I hesitant about shoulder replacement surgery? It's because a search of the literature and the WEB by my surgeon and I have only found five other surgeries on wheelchair users. Mainly because of the high chance of failure of trying to fix something that is usually overused and over destroyed. This was going to be a risky adventure in its own right.

Now it is one day since the surgery. My surgeon told me he achieved 90% success. Dr. Sullivan said the bone mass in my upper shoulder was so far gone there was nothing to attach the appliance to. However, the main prosthesis in my upper arm was successfully installed. The most encouraging thing he told me was that I should be able to transfer and do other things I used to do, but with a 90% reduction in pain.

I did not have to stay in the hospital three days except for Medicare Insurance requirements. If I were not confined to the hospital for three nights, then the cost of the rehabilitation would not be covered. So, three days later on a Friday, I moved to a private rehab facility, (Rennes) to first do more recovery and then start an aggressive therapy program to hopefully lead me back home sooner than later.

Say, this is tedious hitting one key at a time with the wrong hand...I will shoot to post something Sunday from my new digs...Jeff

Posted Jan 31, 2011 5:35am

Today is Sunday the third day in my new quarters. I would have to say overall things are not nearly as bad as I expected. The food is fine and the care is excellent. I sleep a lot and usually up early to watch the sunrise. The staff is surprised that I want my window curtains open at night. I tell them no one wants to peak in and I enjoy watching the night turn to day.

The P.T. & O.T. staff really know what they are doing. I feel I should be able to get out of here in not as long a time as I first thought. I have my own private room. As long as I don't move my shoulder the pain is insignificant. The main reason I am here is because I can exert no pressure on my shoulder which means I cannot move without assistance from slings, winches, powerized wheelchairs and strong backed staff.

I am confined to my bed except for mealtimes. I always have breakfast in bed, but lunch and supper I take in the dining room with the other people who live here. We are assigned a table to sit at. It seems they pair us with others with whom we might get along.

I've had a steady stream of visitors, care staff and therapists, so the time seems to be going by quickly. Jane left today for four days in Las Vegas for a much-needed vacation away from the cold and away from me.

Life at Rennes Rehab Center, week two… the lunchroom and beyond.

Posted Feb 7, 2011 4:15am

As I explained last time, we have assigned tablemates, and mine is Richard. He is a World War 2 veteran who has some mobility problems due to a spinal tap gone badl. He was placed here about 10 days before me and hopes to go home soon. I'm not too sure about that. He and his wife live in a two- story apartment and while he is here his wife has quietly been relocating to a single floor apartment complex where Richard will have easier access. I'm not sure he knows this and I certainly know he is not aware that his wife is disposing of many of his collectables because of limited storage space in the new dwelling.

This is something that all older homeowners are going to face just like death and taxes including Jane and myself. If I can't be rehabbed enough we're also going to have to contemplate selling our home and downsizing. It is very intimidating to have to think about all the stuff we have accumulated over 42 years of marriage and raising a family.

The other thing I learned about Richard from his wife was that he rarely talks about WWII with other people. She is surprised that he has opened up to me about that. Richard was wounded during a beach landing in the South Pacific. My food grew cold while I listened with rapt attention when he told one of his grisly war stories. It was common for Richard to repeat those stories but even then, I still paid attention and responded like I was first hearing the story. (Something that is common with older people as we all have experienced.)

A typical population for a meal is about 5 men and 25 women. I kid Richard about that statistic and that he ought to be cautious about being hit on by one of the ladies! There is a beauty parlor in this place and almost every one of the women has their nails painted and hair coiffed.

You get to order what you want to eat each day for breakfast, lunch and dinner. Lunch is the biggest meal of the day. In addition, on the menu here you can circle if you want a small, medium or large portion of food. You can get just about anything you want to drink but most people have hot chocolate, coffee, milk, water or juice. Once in awhile I order a soda for a change of pace. The food is quite tasty and I have no complaints about it except that I eat too much at least for the minimal amount of exercise I'm doing. One funny thing about the menus is that you fill them out about two to three weeks in advance, which means every meal is a surprise because my brain thinks it is an unimportant item for me to remember.

There is also a lot of the coughing hacking and sneezing going on. Is this where I caught my very infrequent cold? Perhaps!

The dining room is a microcosm of this place with a mixture of disabilities from Alzheimer's to people with knee replacements, from people on oxygen to people who should be on oxygen. You can almost tell who was planning to leave this place to go home and who will leave this place at the end of their lives and go to the hereafter. You can tell it in their eyes. The ones that are here for the duration have a deep level of dullness in their eyes; the shine is gone… what does that say about the hereafter?

We will wrap up this a little tour of the nursing home / rehabilitation center next time with a deeper look at therapy, the staff and other observations.

Life and Death at Rennes … week three

Posted Feb 14, 2011 5:00am

Except for Sundays, I get occupational and physical therapy every day of the week for about a total of 3 hours a day. As of right now I am still in a passive exercise stage which means I can't do any lifting by myself; someone always has to do it for me. I've rented an electric wheelchair with a toggle drive, which allows me a better level of independence. I am able to go places without somebody pushing the wheelchair for me.

I have yet to find any staff person at this place who is grumpy. To a person they're all pleasant and seem really happy to be here helping people like me. And, the therapists are as good as or better than I've ever seen.

And, did I mention the food? There's way too much of it and it is too good. Besides three meals a day there is always a snack cart in the hallway with all sorts of goodies like bags of popcorn, animal crackers, Oreo cookies and pretzels. There's always a jug of cold ice water and anything else that you want to drink on your bedside table. I drink much cranberry juice in an attempt to keep urinary infections at bay.

I have a new level of excitement in my room! A friend of mine, Tom Selk, brought one of our birdfeeders from home and set it up outside my window. I am still however awaiting the first feathered visitor…

Some sadness to report: Both of my tablemates are sick and not doing so well. You recall Richard in my earlier updates. The poor guy is so frail and if I said he looks like death warmed over it would be a positive compliment. Richard now suffers from a bad case of shingles on the right side of his face. It is extremely painful and his right eye is swollen shut. Richard pretty much stays in his room now. Jane and I do go down to try to visit with him

154

once in awhile. In addition, I don't know if I mentioned it that Richard has an elderly brother that lived here as well. I say lived; because Armand passed this past Thursday night.

You've never met my other tablemate Bernice. She is an elderly permanent resident here who only eats lunch with us. She is somewhat mobile in that she has one of the few other electric chairs run by patients here. When I met her she had a terrible cough that I think has transgressed into pneumonia. When I go by her room she's just lying there with a nebulizer mask strapped to her face.

Since my tablemates are absent I've taken to eating at other lunch tables with other residents and trying with limited success to strike up conversations. I say it's limited because in general there are not many conversations going on in the lunchroom. It seems each resident is wrapped up in his or her own thoughts most of the time. And, for others; getting that fork in the mouth takes 100% concentration.

A positive note this past week, I gave a presentation to the residents after supper. It seemed to be well received. My presentation included a short video of one of my climbs. It is a great but short inspirational piece for me and whoever watches it. It's a scenic and breathtaking view of my team climbing and me. At one point it shows my son Chad with me on his back being carried through a very, very narrow but steep passageway near the summit. There were many misty eyes including Jane's and mine.

During the presentation I encouraged the residents to always climb higher. That the outdoors is strong medicine and the value of doing therapy the best they can and to always try to get better at what the therapists want them to do.

The proof came quickly as several therapists the next day told me about marked improvements in some of the residents. One fellow who refused to push his own wheelchair actually pushed himself down to his room from the therapy area. That positive feedback really makes me happy.

Life at Rennes Rehab center/nursing home… week four

Posted Feb 21, 2011 4:00am

Since my tablemates for lunch and dinner are still ill, I moved to a couple different tables and got to know some other people. Now I am back at my original table as I have a new tablemate. He is a younger stroke victim. His name is Jonathan. It is my guess he is probably in his forties and he is so very quiet. When he speaks, it is in a hoarse whisper. He is very nervous and fidgety.

Tuesday night, we had the longest conservation ever. He had a sausage sandwich that he did not want to eat and he asked me if I wanted it. Since I only ordered soup I said sure and thank you. In exchange I gave him my strawberry desert. He accepted and slurped it down. I could tell he also wanted another cup of coffee but was too shy to ask for it; so I so I motioned for a helper to come over and pour him a refill. I had brought along a newspaper sports page to read and he asked if he could read it to. I gave it him and said I already read it even though I had not. Maybe tomorrow we'll even talk more!

Well now it is the next day… This time I brought the entire paper and offered it to Jonathan. He readily accepted it, but kept his mouth shut and went back into his own little world. I am glad Jane had supper with me.

This past Tuesday was the one-month anniversary of my surgery. In addition, I was able to start a new series of exercises that are a little more aggressive. They are still passive but they are still more aggressive than what I was doing. Every time I move my right arm the wrong way, I am reminded why I am in this place. There is no way I could function in the outside world.

Right now I am having therapy in my room because the third wing is in a flu lock down and it is impossible to get to the PT area. It definitely is the flu season and it would be just terrible if that nasty bug spread throughout more of this place.

As you read this what do you think you would do if you were in a place like this? More specifically, what would you do if you were in here for the rest of your life? Would you be all jolly and happy? Would you chat with others as if today is just another day? Would you contemplate your demise? I, have no answers if you ask me those questions. I simply thank Buddha or God that the plan for me is to leave here eventually and in an upright position and not in a hearse.

Well, today is Thursday and for now the flu scare ended. My cousin, Caren Kruger, brought chicken dumpling soup and strawberry ice cream. It was a great dinner with great conversation. Speaking of visitors I play cribbage almost every day with my old, old friend Elmer Schill. Typically we play two games every afternoon; he wins one and I win one. He only lives about three blocks away and walks over here. When he comes in the room, he tosses a bag of popcorn to me that he picked up from the cart in the hallway. I am a popcorn addict!

I see, reading my Care pages responses that, an interest has developed in my tablemates! Well I have some good news to report. Bernice has come out of her room again joining us for lunch and I saw Richard going down the hall the other day with his walker and looking much improved but, Friday, I saw him on the therapy table saying that his face was giving him a great deal of pain.

Life at Rennes Rehab center /nursing home… week five

Posted Feb 28, 2011 3:30am

What a place to get a new phone! I upgraded to a HTC Desire Android and this place affords me the time to figure out how it works. I embrace the new technology as it keeps me out of more trouble than I can handle. I never go anywhere without my cell phone. As I grow older, it has saved me from serious predicaments many times more.

I must be getting cabin fever as I've been planning various adventures for this upcoming summer. I would like to return to Alaska for a week or so of fishing in early August. In addition, I have been invited to be involved in a six-day Apostle Islands kayak trip in late August, which also trips my trigger.

When I told Jane about these possibilities she just rolled her eyes! (Maybe you are rolling your eyes too?)

We had a big snowstorm about a week ago. In the hours before the storm the birdfeeder was doing a great business. Since the storm, I have yet to see any feathered creatures in the backyard outside my window. I am sure the storm did not kill them, but they must have relocated somewhere else and have yet to return. If any of you birds are reading this consider coming back as you provide a significant amount of enjoyment while I sit here!

On Saturday, I did the first weight lift with my new shoulder. It was only 1-pound arm curls but it was a start and another step up the ladder of rehabilitation. It has been a couple stories ago but since I've lauded to the amazing capabilities of my therapists. They are a fantastic bunch. They truly seem to have my best interest in mind and that of my right shoulder. My lead physical therapist has even come to my doctor's appointment so she can make sure she understands his desires on rehabilitation. If you have a therapist, when was the last time they came to your doctor's appointment? See what I mean by amazing?

For me, Tuesdays are somewhat exciting because today is... Shower day! Each Tuesday I'm allowed to take a shower. Thursdays, I get to take a Whirlpool bath. Most residents are allowed only one shower a week but state law allows you to have one every day if you want. I asked for at least two a week. It is quite a process to get wet around here if your legs don't work and you only have one arm that works. If you must know here are the gory details!

First I am stripped in my bed and then lifted by a Hoyer lift to a plastic wheelchair. Then I am covered head to toe with towels and a shroud and wheeled down to the shower room. I get de- shrouded and then I'm allowed to shower myself with a handheld shower nozzle. Feels really good let me tell you. After that, they help dry me off, cover up and back to the room, transferred to the bed and dressed. When it's your only option to get wet, your dignity becomes less important than getting clean. Lest you draw up false illusions please e-mail me if there's some question still remaining in your mind of how I take a shower or the Thursday Whirlpool!

158

An update on Richard. Sadly it's not a good update. He continues to be in lot of pain with the shingles on his face. He does come to the dining room for lunch but eats with his eyes totally closed. This does not surprise me as I have broken bread with many people with visual impairments, so that does not concern me and it does not seem to bother Richard. I describe for him what is on his plate using the clock to pinpoint where his food is. For example, I might say his green beans are at seven o'clock.

What is problematic however is his inability to use his walker or even slightly push his wheelchair. I tried to help him to eat his food yesterday, as he could not lift his fork to his mouth without dropping the morsel back onto the plate or in his lap. In addition, I don't know if it is the drugs but he'll fall asleep right in the middle of eating. Again if I describe his strength as feeble it is an overstatement. I don't know what he or they are going to do to get him stronger so he can go home.

My other tablemate, Jonathon, does not come to the dining room anymore at I believe the urging of the staff. Due to his disability or perhaps just the flu; he can't keep his food down no matter how many times he tries to shove it down his throat. As a result of that my wife, Jane, does not want to eat in the dining room anymore. I can't really blame her.

To conclude this week's report I need to reiterate that no one wants to be in this place. Because of that there is a base layer of sadness that is very thick. In addition, no matter how many cherry volunteers there are, no matter how good the food might be, no matter how great the staff is and everything else that is positive about this place, it is still very sad and colors my comments in a dull shade of gray.

Coming next week… the volunteers and me.

Life at Rennes Rehab center /nursing home… Week Six

Posted March 6, 2011 5:30am

I don't think anyone has stated that this log is for the birds but one or two of them must have read last week's report as I am now getting visits to the bird feeder. I even had a gray squirrel show up one day. I don't mind that as there is plenty of sunflower seed to go around. Then, in the dark, a big ol rabbit cleans up what the messy squirrel dropped on snow.

Last week I volunteered to become a volunteer here at the nursing home. I even have my own name badge. My duties include the following: On certain Monday's and Thursdays I call bingo. I was told that it is a can't win situation. Some people will say I'd talk too fast and others will say I'd talk too slow. I am happy to report that I got no complaints at my first attempt at bingo calling.

 I'm also the community Gardner. They have a little raised gardening bed in the activity room. This past weekend three of my grandchildren helped me plant peas and lettuce. I figured I should grow a crop that can be easily eaten without cooking. In only seven days the lettuce is about ½ inch tall and the first of the peas are also breaking ground. For the first time today I turned on the artificial lighting.

I also help the volunteer coordinator keep track of volunteer hours. That one is a tedious job that just cries out for a computer spreadsheet. I need to convince the coordinator to come into the cyberspace age. Well, I had no luck convincing her. She said "wait until I retire and the next person takes over!"

I get my weight checked every Tuesday and Thursday before getting wet. It is not a good time as I know I am eating too much and checking my weight is a reality check. Since I've been here I have gained 9 pounds. This weight gain is going to work against me when it becomes time to start transferring from my chair to other things. So reluctantly I am going to start calorie counting once again. I did this a year ago and I lost 47 pounds and I was maintaining quite well until I got here. Therefore, the first day of my calorie-counting program finds me weighing 189 pounds. I want to get back under 180 as soon as I can. To do this I can no longer eat more than 2,000 calories a day. Even at that intake dropping pounds will be tough without much physical exercise, but I have to try.

Surprise, surprise, all of my table mates are back at the lunch table. So far so good with Jonathan as he has not so much as burped! In addition, Richard, can open both eyes but still is very weak and slow. And Bernice, well she's just a hoot. Her food comes, she stares at it, (she is so short her head just comes right to the top of the table) rolls her eyes, and shoves the plate away. She does eat the desert if one is provided and nutritional wise she looks just fine.

This coming Monday, March 14 is an important day for me. It is appointment day with my surgeon. I hope he allows me to get rid of this electric wheelchair and start using my power assist chair again. That will be another major step in my rehabilitation process. The power assist care is also battery powered but it will allow me to push with both arms but with not a lot of stress of my right arm. I will let you all know next week if I was successful.

The only complaint I have about all the fresh snow we're getting is that I cannot ski this winter. But what a winter it must've been for skiing around Green Bay; it seems we have had some snow forever. And, when you see what is happening around the world it's kind of nice to be from good old Green Bay were the only complaint now is wondering when spring will show will up.

Today I learned something watching the wildlife outside my window. It's Friday and it's bright sunshine. I've had the most birds ever at my feeder plus Mr. Squirrel. Today I had mourning doves, sparrows and chickadees. I still don't have a problem with Mr. Squirrel eating the birdseed as there is plenty to go around. I understand now Mr. Squirrel's sloppy eating habits also benefits Mr. Rabbit. He is out there after dark eating all the sunflower seeds that drop down to the snow. He does a fine job cleaning up and he gets some nutrition to boot. What a simple but interesting relationship between wild creatures.

Today was the day we were supposed to fly to San Diego and jump on a cruise ship for a ten-day cruise to Hawaii and back. We of course had to cancel and have saved our spot on the ship for this time next year. However, somebody forgot to cancel the hotel and airline reservations we had. The hotel was no big deal as we did not have to pay any money down but we did buy the airline tickets ahead of time. We were forced between two options of losing all that money or finding a different place to go before July 22 and use the tickets. So…Jane and I are spending five days in New York City during the 4th of July week. Therefore, that is another thing to plan for and to dream about as I wait my escape from this place. Our hotel is right next to Times Square so maybe one day you'll see us waving from the crowd at the Today Show!

In closing for this week, thank you to all my visitors that shorten the days. Thank you for all the positive comments on the care page site, my face book site and plain old-fashioned e-mail! See you next week…

Life at Rennes Week Seven

Posted Feb 15, 2011 5:00am

Well, I had my appointment with my Dr. Sullivan this past Monday morning. Once again my therapist came with. The doctor had good news and bad news, I guess. First he told me I shouldn't try using my power assist wheelchair but to stay with the electric chair. The electric chair is heavy and cumbersome in tight places. It is particularly difficult to use around the house especially getting into my elevator. I should clear up that by now, I am allowed brief forays outside Rennes. I got to the doctor's office and stopped at home to take care of some paperwork I could only access on my home computer.

He said this is a critical time and I need to take it slow and not push, figuratively and literally. This is kind of frustrating as I am getting anxious for more activity. But, he felt confident I would still out of here by the middle of April or earlier. He did tell my therapists that I could start next week to attempt transfers using a sliding board. Once I master transferring, like from my wheelchair to the shower chair or from my wheelchair to my bed I will be able to leave this place. My right arm is still very weak and this will be a tough nut to crack. So I continue to work on strengthening exercises for both of my arms. I am pretty sure the left arm is ready to go; it is just the right arm, which is so weak.

The birds continue to use my bird feeder as does Mr. Squirrel and Mr. Rabbit. My bingo calling is going well with no complaints to date. The garden my grandkids and I planted is coming up nicely. I have been taking pictures and sending them to the kids so they can see the progress.

I can see why people in their spare time are constantly looking at their high technology cell phones. I am slowly mastering my HTC Android. It is a fascinating piece of electronic technology.

There is this delightful elderly lady that eats at the table next to mine. She always wears her hair in a bun except one time in the hallway I saw her in her wheelchair with her hair down. She must weigh all of 85 pounds. She is very quiet and she eats very slowly. And, she has this perpetual nose drip. It turns out that she is the oldest resident in this place at 106!

My table mate Richard seems to be slowly bouncing back once again. He still suffers from shingles on his face but he seems to have a little bit more energy. They have rented a new apartment that is all on one floor and the move is to happen in two weeks. Richard's wife's problem is that his insurance ran out about Valentine's Day. So each day is at least another $200. That is really starting to add up.

My other table mate Jonathan does not come to the dining room at all anymore. His name is even off the table label that designates who sits where. We, meaning Jane or one of my friends usually drops off the daily newspaper at his room after we're done reading it. Jonathan still welcomes that little perk.

This is now early Thursday morning, and it has been a long night for my next door neighbor, Johan. He is a very elderly man with dementia and has been at this place for over five years. Once in awhile over the past weeks he can't find his call button and then yells for help. Moreover, when no one comes he starts banging on the wall, bedrail or whatever he can reach. When Jane is here she will go into the room to see what she can do as I would do if I am in my wheelchair. Some nights when I am already in bed, I would push my call light so when the staff comes down I re-direct them to his room. Last night the yelling and banging started early and continued almost all night. Apparently Johan was in a lot of pain and had nightmares.

The staff is doing what they can but as soon as they leave the room he would start yelling again. Periodically he would be quiet and you knew the medications they were giving him were working to settle him down. I feel very helpless and that all I can do is ring my call light when it sounds like he's not getting the attention he is clamoring for. Last night was the worst it's ever been.

Now it's Friday morning and a brief update about Johan. All was quiet last night so both of us must have rested well. But, a casualty of the warm weather outside is my birdfeeder tipped over... help!

As of Friday morning the third wing is again under quarantine with another outbreak of influenza. This past Monday I was diagnosed with another UTI so I do not know whether to attribute my body aches to the flu or truly a urinary infection. Either way it seems to be getting better, this on my seventh week anniversary.

The maintenance man reset my fallen bird feeder. To date I have now had at least 10 different species of birds who have visited me outside my window. (House sparrow, crow, junco, chickadee, mallard, starling, robin, cardinal, red winged blackbird and mourning dove.) Even though snow is in the forecast for next week you can just tell Mother Spring is about to be reborn. Thank you for letting me share my story with you all!

Life at Rennes Week 8

Posted March 22, 2011 4:10am

Preparations continue for my departure on April fool's day. I suppose this could be a sign that I might be leaving here too early in my rehabilitation. But, in my heart I feel confident that it is the right decision.

Next week, I will restart sessions with occupational therapists as well as continuing with my physical therapy. The O.T. people will work on my independent living skills to make sure I will be able to take care of myself when I am home. Those skills will concentrate on dressing and my biggest problem of all, which is pulling my pants up over my butt! I can fairly easily get the left side up but it's the right side that gives me fits.

And no, I can't expect Jane to help with any of this. I already hurt her once last fall that required her to get a shoulder scope and long and painful rehabilitation for herself. Nope, I need to be able to do all the stuff on my own.

It's starting to become common knowledge around here that I will be leaving here soon. At first, I would share this information with anyone who was listening but right now I am not. Especially with those that are here forever. While I get to go home and resume my life they have to stay here until they die. That is not a very pleasant thought so I will now start to keep my happiness about leaving to myself and of course my Care Page readers!

After last week's record setting snowstorm the birds really crowd into my feeder. It does not look like very many of them flew back south to regroup. I guess I am somewhat like those birds in that I am ready to head out even though there are certain signs that say it is too early to do that. Does that make me a birdbrain?

Although it's not probably not the fault of any one person or any one policy, places like this that have people living in close proximity to each other are great places for bugs to grow and or disease to spread. I have said earlier that I rarely get the common cold. Now I've been here just eight weeks and I am nurturing my second common cold since I've been here. That is becoming too "common".

I'm certainly glad I got a flu shot last fall as I believe it is helping me stay healthy in that respect. There is a lot of flu also going on around here. In addition, on Thursday I received a Shingles vaccination. Some people say Shingles is infectious and others say it is not. Everyone agrees it is nasty and painful disease. However, the general medical theory is that people over the age of 60 should get the vaccine. Therefore, I got it.

This weekend is moving time for Richard's family. As you recall they're moving from a two story to a single story home. I am afraid it was a missed goal in that Richard still cannot leave this place. I'm afraid his dementia is getting worse. I hope I am wrong.

I wanted to say something about the relatives and friends that frequent this place. Pat is a woman down the hall who had a brain aneurysm almost two years ago. She is never without a family member during the daylight hours.

There is always someone with her as the rehabilitative process goes on and on and on.

Especially on weekends, there are many families here visiting with loved ones. In addition, there are many pets. Jane brings Molli, our English Springer Spaniel at least once a week so she remembers me when I get home. I myself have been blessed with Jane coming every day as well as many, many friends.

By my rough guess, only a little bit more than 50% of the patients here see visitors. If you know someone in a nursing home, please go see him or her. Having visitors sure makes a person feel wanted which I have learned is a basic human need. Think spring!

And now, the final chapter at Rennes...

Posted Apr 3, 2011 11:42am

As planned, I was able to leave Rennes on Friday April Fool's Day at 9:30am when Son Corey picked me up. It was a happy/sad situation. Saying goodbye to the staff that nursed me back to health was bittersweet. There were many good by hugs and "see ya later" comments.

I have been home three days now with mixed results. For the most part, I have been able to take care of myself on my own. It was great being able to sleep in my own bed, take showers and prepare food. (Tonight it's going to be an entire chicken on the grill with fresh veggies.)

However, later last night I got all achy and not just the wounded shoulder. Makes me think I am becoming susceptible to changes in weather conditions. Can those theories be true? Now, this morning, we are getting another snow thunderstorm. However, I do feel a bit less achy.

So, maybe yesterday I over did it or I can blame the weather. Either way, I will just concentrate more on passive chores rather than the physical ones that need to be done. I do at least know I can push my power assist wheelchair, so I can abandon the totally electric chair. I also found out yesterday, I am able to drive my car as well as get in and out of it. So, normalcy is returning.

This care pages site has served us all well but I think it's time to stop the weekly updates. Let's all of us do our best to keep in touch as life moves on and on. All for now, Jeff.

Chapter 25 - Deep Doo Doo Stories

This chapter consists of some strange but true stories of things that happened to me or I caused to happen to me throughout my career. I did not know where else to mention them so I created a chapter right here just for them. Finger licking chicken rewards that I mentioned in an earlier chapter reminds me of another story of finger licking rewards.

This story happened when I was working for the Wisconsin Department Natural Resources. We had a staff meeting up north in the small town of Woodruff. I fished a lake nearby called Little Arbor Vitae. I fished that water body often with Tom Wilson.

The staff meeting lasted for three days and ended about noon on Friday. I brought a little 14-foot boat along and a brand new 15-horse Mercury outboard motor. I was proud of that motor because it was the first new outboard motor I ever owned. I planned to go fishing on Little Arbor Vitae with one of my able bodied co-workers after the meeting ended before heading back to Green Bay.

As the time neared to fish, the co-worker informed me that his plans had changed and he could not go. But he said he could help me launch my boat if I wanted to still go by myself. I accepted his offer and we drove to the boat landing. He helped me get into my boat and away I went.

Because of rain showers and a brisk northeast wind, it was actually a miserable day for boating and fishing. I caught just a few small perch before deciding to head home. As I motored back to the boat landing I could see it was deserted. It looked like I was going to have to load the boat by myself. What happened next was a comedy of errors that didn't quit until five hours later when I was back in Green Bay.

I was able to get out of the boat OK and get in the wheelchair on the dock and push to my van in the parking lot. Back in those days, I would jump into the passenger side of the van, pull the chair in behind me and shut the sliding door. Finally I would jump across the seat to the driver's position and drive away. Because I was going just a short distance, I left side door open. When I drove down to the boat ramp, I made a tight turn to line the trailer up with the ramp. When I did, the turn centrifugal force and gravity caused my wheelchair to fly out the open side door careening along the blacktop before finally coming to rest. Did I mention there was no one at this boat landing that could help out?

I was able to maneuver the van up near the wheelchair and reach over with a stick to pull it back into the van. I resumed backing the rig down to the water's edge to load the boat. I got to what I thought was the right position. I slid across the seat, pulled out the chair and dropped into it. It was not until I rolled down the ramp and onto the dock and undid the mooring line that I realized that I had not backed the trailer far enough into the water. So I retied the boat, pushed myself back up to the van got into the front passenger seat, pulled in my chair and jumped across the seat, started the van and readjusted my position. It took me three times doing this sequence before I got it right. The third time was the charm. I pushed on the dock, undid the mooring and hooked the boat to the trailer line. Now, all I had to do was push up around the front of the car, drop down the other side and crank the boat on to the trailer.

When I got down on the other side I saw that tragedy struck. Somehow I had not secured the hook to the boat very well and it had come off. The boat with the new motor was slowly drifting away from the landing. And, did I mention there was no one else around?

I quickly stripped off my shoes and shirt, plunked down onto the ramp, and butted myself into the water. Burr it was cold. Also, did I mention I swim like a six year old?

The boat was picking up speed and was now about 15 feet from the shore and there was about a mile of open water before it would smash into the rocky, windswept shore. I struck out after my boat and eventually caught it about 50 yards from shore. I hung on the boat resting for a minute as the wind kept pushing me further away from a ramp. I was able to reach a line hanging from the boat. I put the line in my teeth and started breast stroking back to the landing. It took about 20 minutes to get back to shallow water and fully secure the boat. I did this by sitting in the water near the water's edge. I cranked the boat up and secured it to the trailer. I was much stronger then and I was able to vault back into my wheelchair - something I can no longer do. I pushed up around the front of the van, hoisted myself back into the passenger seat, loaded the wheelchair, started the motor, and drove away. Just then another rig pulled into the parking lot. Timing is everything!

That is not the end of the story. I drove through Woodruff and turned into a Kentucky Fried Chicken place. I had decided to reward myself for the recent trials and tribulations by eating some greasy chicken. I ordered a large cup of soda and a three-piece meal with mashed potatoes and coleslaw. As I am prone to do I started driving while munching on the chicken. I did not realize that when my greasy hand tried to grasp the soda it slipped through my fingers to the floor re-dousing my already cold and wet feet once again. Some days are like that with nothing that goes as planned. As with most "deep doo doo" stories, they were not funny at the time but the humor grew as time marched on.

A header off the bridge and dirty pants

In the early 1990's part of my job with the State of Wisconsin involved patrolling public snowmobile trails in northeast Wisconsin. Many times I hauled my sit ski along and skied after riding the snow machine for six to eight hours. I was in Florence County, which is up north on the border between Wisconsin and Upper Michigan. The county is heavily forested with very few residents. I choose a ski trail loop on the Nicolet National Forest. There was no one in the parking lot and as is typical in northern Wisconsin in deep winter, there were several feet of snow on the ground. The looped trail was about three miles long and single tracked probably by a volunteer on a snowmobile. There was about an hour of daylight left.

I had only skied several hundred yards when I came to a bridge across a small still running trout stream. The rushing water was shallow but gurgling merrily as it swept under a bridge. What I did not realize was how narrow the bridge was. As I poled across the bridge my left pole stuck through the snow into thin air. Momentum carried me almost across the bridge but not quite. I slid about four feet down the steep bank and the tails of my skis rested on the bottom of the stream. The ski tips just about reached the trail. I was looking up at about a 45 degree angle. What a pickle I had got myself into again!

I strap myself into the sit ski with three belts. One around the waist, one around the knees and one around the ankles. I strained to try and ski myself out of the ditch but did not move an inch. I could not plant the poles in the soft snow and the grade was too steep. So, my next idea was to undo the straps. Nothing happened when I released the ankle strap, but when I released the knee strap my entire lower body slid downward and into the creek. I was able to undo the waist belt without falling any more into the frigid water. I then used one of my poles to shovel away the deep unpacked snow between where I was sitting and the trail. After about 20 minutes with a makeshift snow shovel I had cleared a route back up to the ski trail.

I then started an arduous climb back up to the trail only four feet above, but it might as well have been 400 feet. I was making progress, about an inch at a time, butting myself backwards up the hill. (I don't want to leave you hanging, but I must digress for a paragraph.)

When able-bodied people see someone in a wheelchair, the usual first reaction is some level of pity for the chair user because they have lost the ability to walk. Let me tell you that for most chair users the ability to walk is down a ways on the list of lost functions. High on the list is the inability to control ones bowel and bladder.

About halfway up, the four-foot climb the intense straining caused an unintended result. An overpowering stench pervaded the cold crisp air coming with the advancing darkness. "Just great" I muttered to myself as I finally reached the trail and got back on the sit ski. As the evening shadows lengthened, I could make out a dark brown streak the last two feet of my backwards climb.

I did not dare to try to re-cross the bridge so I still had almost three miles to get back to the van. I had brought no flashlight but a rising moon lit the way back. Except for the soiled ski pants and odor the remaining ski would have been a neat adventure. On my long drive back home to Green Bay I had the heaters turned on full blast but the windows wide open.

Stuck on a stump with my ATV

Sometimes I hunt deer and other critters with the use of an All Terrain Vehicle, (ATV). Sometimes I hoist my wheelchair on the back and take it along and sometimes I don't. One day during the gun deer hunting season I left the chair back at the cabin because I did not expect be gone that long. I was driving through a managed pine plantation. I needed to be careful to avoid high centering the ATV on any of the many hidden stumps in the plantation. Apparently I was not careful enough because I did end up high centered on a stump. No matter how I rocked the ATV all four tires spun uselessly in the air.

I easily slid off the ATV onto the relatively soft forest floor. (Here, the law of gravity was in my favor, later trying to climb back up it worked against me.) I dragged myself to the front of the machine where to get a better angle at the stump. In my little ditty bag, I was lucky enough to have brought along a hatchet, knife and screwdriver.

With the tools, I set to work chipping and hacking at the stump. It was slow work and took about two hours before I was able to rock the ATV off the stump and get all four tires back on the ground. Now, I had to pull myself back up on the ATV and yes, if you guessed that I had to head back to the cabin for a new pair of underwear, you are correct!

A cold, cold story

January 21st, 2013 was a Monday, and what do we usually do on Mondays? We go fishing. Even though the temperature hovered around seven and the winds blew the wind chill down to more than -20 we still "had" to go ice fishing. We targeted a 220-acre lake near Laona that held Musky, Northerns, Bass and Pan fish.

Jim Kleist and I picked up Steve Redmann at 5:30 am in Cecil. My mini-van heater was working overtime all the way from Green Bay.

We arrived at the parking lot leading to the lake about daybreak and quickly unloaded the gear and hooked my ATV up to the trailer we used to haul the ATV. My wheelchair was secured to the heap and we were ready to go…except the ATV would not start. It was dying of a dead battery for sure. However, I had brought along a smallish battery starter and we hooked it up. Bingo, the ATV roared to life.

To get to our target lake, we had to cross another huge lake. The ice was thick judging by all the other machine tracks in the snow. It was about a 2-mile ride into the wind, we had to stop several times to adjust facemasks, and gloves to warm up exposed skin. We all had hand warmers, which were very much a blessing.

The trail at the end of this lake twisted into the woods and it was too narrow, thus we had to leave the big trailer behind. It took two trips to transfer all our ice fishing gear including the three of us, a tent, and bait, fishing gear, ice drill and heaters. Of course, the "hot spot" was on the far end of the lake, so the total distance from the van was over 4 miles.

Steve and Jim quickly drilled holes for tip ups and set up the tent. My job was to try to hold the tent in place from the inside until the other guys could pin it in place. It did not take long and we were fishing. It was not too bad in the tent with the three of us and a propane heater. By not too bad, I mean we could take our mittens off and not suffer frostbite.

Soon it was lunchtime and we enjoyed Steve's famous but frozen bologna and cheese sandwiches and slushy cans of soda with cherry pie heated on the propane frame for dessert. Fishing was slow with a small one brought up out of the fishing holes once in awhile. Twice, a bell sounded outside indicating a tip up had gone off. Each time, a nice fat Northern Pike was soon flopping on the ice. However, it did not take long before the fish were frozen pretty much solid.

About 3:00 pm, with two hours of daylight remaining, we agreed it was time to pack up and get off the lake even if it is a well-known fact that fish might bite better as daylight wanes. We all were getting colder and colder.

Here is where the deep dodo part comes in! We could not get the ATV to start. We tried the small battery jumper and it almost started. We pulled and pulled the starter rope without success. We had not yet taken the tent down, so Jim and Steve dragged it over to the ATV and put the tent over it. We had two heaters along and we put those under the ATV to assist in attempting to warm it up.

Somehow, all three of us also managed to fit in the tent. A warm, moist fog bank was inside the tent, but no one was complaining considering the alternative of being outside. The wind started to blow even harder as the sun got lower in the western sky.

After about a half hour of trying to warm up the ATV, we figured we had one kick left out of the charger, so the plan was for Jim to start the motor with the charger, electric start and choke while Steve pulled the starter rope and I managed the throttle.

At the count of three, we all started our respective tasks with little success. The motor almost started but did not. Steve kept pulling with all his might at the balky starter rope. We could hear the electric starter "clicking" which indicated the battery was not delivering enough juice. Then...yes, the motor putted twice and then three times and then four more times before finally roaring to life! I kept pumping the throttle making sure to give it just enough gas to keep running and not flooding.

Steve and Jim made quick work of packing up the gear. They both helped me up on the ATV and Jim and I took off with our first load to the trailer on the other lake. By the time we reached the trailer, unloaded and started back, Steve had already walked off the lake and was in the woods. That was smart of him, because it allowed him to warm up with the exercise.

Jim sat on the front of the ATV and became a windbreak for me, as my face was really getting cold. He was if not a lifesaver, a face saver. As darkness settled in, we retrieved the remaining gear on the lake and headed once again back to the trailer. After the gear was transferred, we quickly motored back across the big first lake to my van on the far side. I noticed for the first time, the ATV gas tank needle was registering on empty, but we never had to switch to the reserve tank.

I got in the car's driver seat, started the motor, and tried to patiently wait for the heater to heat. I was somewhat worried that the parts of my body I could not feel, (tummy on down) might have suffered frostbite or worse. I glanced at the cars outside thermometer, it registered minus nine.

Three hours later, I lay nervously on the bed at home and peeled off layers and layers of pants and socks. Thankfully, I had dressed in warm layers and my feet and legs were nice, warm, and pink. No damage. Just more memories to re-live around the dinner table and other places.

Well, it is time to close in on the end of this task of writing a book. It was a tough chore and I am duly impressed with anyone who has seen his or her work published. I hope that I too will see this work also published.

My parting words are similar to my beginning ones. The Great Outdoors is truly a magic place that will improve your well-being in so many different ways. Even if you don't feel so good and are just sitting around, sitting outside will improve whatever is not feeling good at the time. Moreover, while my actual mountain climbing days are over, the memories will never cease.

In addition, I can continue to climb higher in different ways. If I take my hand bike out for a ride, I still try to go farther than I did the time before. And, if I am at the gym and lift a weight ten times, the next time I try to lift it eleven times and the next time twelve.

No matter who you are, or what your physical abilities might be, I encourage each and every reader to find ways to do the same. Make life a competition with yourself and you will reap great benefits from striving to do a little more every day and in every way.

Always, always climb higher!

THE END

Made in the USA
Charleston, SC
25 October 2014